THE
TRADITIONS
OF
CHRISTMAS

THE TRADITIONS OF CHRISTMAS

EDITED BY NANCY J. SKARMEAS

IDEALS PUBLICATIONS
NASHVILLE, TENNESSEE

ISBN 0-8249-4127-6

Library of Congress Cataloging-in-Publication Data
The traditions of Christmas / edited by Nancy J. Skarmeas. — 1st ed.
     p.   cm.
  Includes index.
  ISBN 0-8249-4127-6
  1. Christmas—United States. 2. Jesus Christ—Nativity.
3. United States—Social life and customs. I. Skarmeas, Nancy J.
GT4986.A1T73   1997
394.2667'0973—DC21   97-31560
                      CIP

Publisher, Patricia A. Pingry
Associate Editor, Michelle Prater Burke
Book Designer, Tina Wells Davenport
Editorial Assistant, Tara E. Lynn

Printed and bound in Italy
Color film separations by Precision Color Graphics

Published by Ideals Publications, a division of Guideposts
535 Metroplex Drive, Suite 250
Nashville, Tennessee 37211

10 9 8 7 6 5 4 3 2

ACKNOWLEDGMENTS

Ideals Publications Incorporated has made every effort to trace
the ownership of all copyrighted material. Thanks are due to
the following authors, publishers, and agents for permission to
use the material indicated:

Bowen, Elizabeth, "Home for Christmas." Reprinted by per-
mission of Curtis Brown, Ltd., London.
Del Re, Gerard and Patricia, "The Messiah." From *The
Christmas Almanack,* copyright © 1979 by Gerard and
Patricia Del Re.
Engle, Paul, "On the Farm." From *An Old Fashioned Christmas,*
copyright © 1964 by Paul Engle and Eleanor Pownall
Simmons.
Henderson, Yorke, "Bethlehem" and "The Star." From "The
First Christmas" from *Parents' Magazine's Christmas
Holiday Book,* copyright © 1972 by Parents' Magazine
Press. Reprinted by permission of Scholastic Inc.
Krythe, Maymie Richardson, "England's Great Christmas"
and "Good Saint Nick." From *All About Christmas,* copy-
right © 1954 by Maymie Richardson Krythe. Used by
permission of HarperCollins Publishers.
McGinley, Phyllis, "The Ballad of Befana." Copyright © 1957
by Phyllis McGinley. First appeared in *Good
Housekeeping.* Published by *Good Housekeeping.*
Reprinted by permission of Curtis Brown, Ltd.
Storey, Violet Alleyn, "Christmas Trees." Published by *Good
Housekeeping.* Reprinted by permission of Abingdon
Press.

Our sincere thanks to the following authors whom we were
unable to contact: W. Bardsley Brash for "The Boy without a
Name"; Clarence Hawkes for "The Gift"; Alfred Carl Hottes
for "The Wise Men from the East"; Edith King for "The
Holly"; Marguerite Merington for "Christmas Eve"; John N.
Then for "The Gift of Bethlehem" and "A Lamb Conceals the
Christ Child"; and Vera E. Walker for "Legend of the Flight
into Egypt."

Cover Illustration: *The Christmas Tree,* Albert Chevallier Tayler, 1862–1925.
Title Page Illustration: *Village in Winter,* Frans De Momper, 1630–1660.

Contents

Come, sing a hale Heigh-ho
For the Christmas long ago!—
When the old log-cabin homed us
From the night of blinding snow,
Where the rarest joy held reign,
And the chimney roared amain,
With the firelight like a beacon
Through the frosty window-pane.

—James Whitcomb Riley

CHRISTMAS BEGINNINGS

And it came to pass in those days, that there went out a decree from Caesar Augustus, that all the world should be taxed. And all went to be taxed, every one into his own city.

—Luke 2:1, 3

A t the root of every Christmas celebration, every tradition, and every custom is the story of the birth of Jesus. Whether told in the simple words of the Gospels of Luke and Matthew or in any of the countless beautiful legends and stories that have grown out of the events in the Bethlehem manger, it is in the Christmas story that the true meaning of Christmas lies.

The Census at Bethlehem, Pieter Brueghel the Younger. In this interpretation of the census at Bethlehem, Brueghel places the census in a typical sixteenth-century Dutch peasant village.

But thou, Bethlehem Ephratah, though thou be little among the thousands of Judah, yet out of thee shall he come forth unto me that is to be ruler in Israel;

THE COMING MESSIAH

From the beginning of their history, the Jewish people were told by men they called prophets of a Messiah who would one day come and transform their world, a Saviour who would gather a new community of believers and create a kingdom of God on earth, a kingdom that recognized no boundaries of nationality or race. The vision of the prophets was cumulative; together over the generations their words created the image of the Saviour whom Christians would come to know as Jesus Christ.

The prophets were a special group of believers, generally young and radical minded. Their words were not always warmly embraced by the people. They called for repentance and chastised the rich and privileged, and some of them told the Israelites that God did not belong to them alone. But the prophets' words were also full of beauty and hope. The prophet Daniel told of the "Son of man" arriving on "the clouds of heaven." Isaiah, a prophet and poet, a counsellor to kings, wrote of the Messiah as the light who would brighten a world grown dark. He described the Saviour in the most glorious terms:

> For unto us a child is born,
> unto us a son is given:
> and the government shall be upon his shoulder:
> and his name shall be called Wonderful, Counsellor,
> The mighty God, The everlasting Father,
> The Prince of Peace (Isaiah 9:6).

Isaiah's words were familiar to the Jews who lived under Herod, the very Jews blessed to be among those whose lifetime was touched by the birth of the long foretold Messiah. So long had they heard of the great One to come, so glowingly had they heard Him described; yet many never noticed the Baby born to humble parents in the tiny Bethlehem manger. How could such a simple Child fulfill the grand prophecies of old; how could one of their own also be the long awaited Prince of Peace?

whose
goings forth
have been
from of
old,
from
everlasting.

—Micah 5:2

MARY AND JOSEPH

Pamela Kennedy

As
Joseph was
a-walking,
He heard an
angel
sing,
"This night
shall be the
birth-time
Of
Christ,
the heavenly
king.

Passage to Bethlehem, Anton Becker.

M ary closed her eyes wearily and sighed, finding it difficult to breathe deeply with the weight of her unborn child pressing upon her. The hot sun scorched her skin, and the gritty desert dust sifted into the folds of her robe. It had seemed an adventure at first, setting off for the city of David with Joseph. It would be a welcome break from the stares and gossip of Nazareth's narrow streets. But now she wondered. Her mother's glare of disapproval as they left home was still vivid in Mary's mind. . . . She sighed again and opened her burning eyes. . . .

"You have been so strong, my little one," he said softly, and she rewarded his kind words with a tired smile. "I think tonight we may reach Bethlehem. It should be just over that far rise there." . . .

The white sun finally started its descent across the western sky, and a breeze came up, refreshing the weary couple. . . . The sky was quickly darkening and already Mary could see the early stars. Their brightness seemed exaggerated in the cooling air, and one stood brilliantly over the city itself. Its beauty captured Mary's attention and she called to Joseph, "See the star, Joseph! It is as if God lights our way!"

Joseph turned and grinned at her. "Your relief at reaching Bethlehem has turned you into a poet, Mary!" he teased. . . .

Joseph stopped several travelers to inquire about directions to an inn. . . . Mary overheard the words, "full, crowded, no room," and her shoulders dropped. Still, Joseph continued, stopping, inquiring, knocking on door after door. . . . They stopped at three more places and were leaving the third when the wife of the innkeeper ran after them and pulled on Joseph's sleeve.

"Is your wife with child?" she asked, concern clouding her plump features.

"Yes and about to deliver, I fear," Joseph replied.

"Come," the woman insisted and led them around the side of the inn to a small cave-like enclosure where the animals were stabled for the night. "It isn't much," she said softly, regret filling her voice, "but it will be clean and quiet." Efficiently, she set about heaping clean straw in a vacant corner, then she removed her shawl and arranged it over the soft, sweet bed. "Put her here and tie the donkey outside," she ordered, at ease in charge of things. . . .

Mary grimaced with pain and the older woman smoothed the hair from her forehead. "There, there now, little one. You will do fine and soon you will have a bouncing baby to hold in your arms." Her manner was reassuring and Mary felt calm. . . .

When the child came at last, the woman wrapped him in the cloths Joseph had brought and laid him at his mother's breast. Exhausted and exultant, Mary studied the tiny face, the pursing lips, the age-old newborn eyes, and the babe sighed and nuzzled close. She traced the flawless cheek with her finger and pondered as she held her slumbering son. Her mind could not grasp it all, but her mother's heart, awakened by the Spirit of the Living God, began to comprehend this culminating work of love. She gazed upon her child and saw her Father's will. For him, she knew, the journey was just beginning.

"He neither shall be born In housen nor in hall, Nor in the place of Paradise, But in an ox's stall.

A CHRISTMAS HYMN

Alfred Domett

It was the calm and silent night!
  Seven hundred years and fifty-three
Had Rome been growing up to might,
  And now was Queen of land and sea.
No sound was heard of clashing wars;
  Peace brooded o'er the hush'd domain;
Apollo, Pallas, Jove and Mars,
  Held undisturb'd their ancient reign,
    In the solemn midnight
      Centuries ago.

O strange indifference!—low and high
  Drows'd over common joys and cares:
The earth was still—but knew not why;
  The world was listening—unawares.
How calm a moment may precede
  One that shall thrill the world for ever!
To that still moment none would heed,
  Man's doom was link'd, no more to sever,
    In the solemn midnight
      Centuries ago.

It *is* the calm and solemn night!
  A thousand bells ring out, and throw
Their joyous peals abroad, and smite
  The darkness, charm'd and holy now.
The night that erst no name had worn,
  To it a happy name is given;
For in that stable lay new-born
  The peaceful Prince of Earth and Heaven,
    In the solemn midnight
      Centuries ago.

"He neither shall be clothed In **purple** nor in pall, But in the fair white **linen** That usen babies **all.**

Opposite: *Adorazione del Bambino*,
Antonio Allegri Correggio,
1489–1534.

"He neither shall be rockèd In silver nor in gold, But in a wooden manger That resteth on the mould."

Bethlehem

Yorke Henderson

As Joseph was a-walking, There did an **angel** sing, And Mary's child at **midnight** Was born to be our **King.**

From Nazareth to Bethlehem is about seventy miles in a straight line. But the road between those two small Jewish communities was anything but straight, so that the journey was hard and long and could take even an able-bodied man nearly a week. To a pregnant young woman who had probably never been away from her native village, the journey must have seemed interminable and frightening. . . .

The times were troubled and violent in any case, and travelling was not undertaken lightly. It had been sixty years since the Romans under their great general Pompey had crushed Jewish resistance and added the coastal lands of the Eastern Mediterranean to their empire; and thirty years had passed since their puppet Herod had been placed on the throne in Jerusalem. Nevertheless, rebellion still simmered just below the surface. In secret places among the hills, armed men waited restlessly for the Messiah who, the old prophets had promised, would come to deliver the Jews from their oppressors. Indeed, it was from the very town of Bethlehem, toward which the Nazarene carpenter and his wife were going, that the prophet Micah seven hundred years earlier had said that the Messiah would come: "You, Bethlehem, in the land of Judah, are not by any means the least among the rulers of Judah; for from you will come a leader who will guide my people Israel."

The old prophecies also said that the deliverer would be a Nazarene. But the child who was soon to be born in Bethlehem was not the kind of leader awaited by the men of the resistance. Their Messiah was to be another Joshua or Gideon or Judas Maccabaeus, a mighty warrior with the wrath of God in his sword arm. Such concerns, however, were not for Joseph and his young wife struggling toward Bethlehem. They were humble people who knew nothing of politics, and who would be grateful when they were done with the tiresome business of registering with the census-takers in Bethlehem. They had to travel to Bethlehem because Joseph was a "descendant of David." Under the old Jewish tribal system, he belonged to the same clan as the great warrior king who had slain Goliath, and consequently his home town was the same as David's—Bethlehem. The Roman overlords taxed their subject peoples heavily, and, being bureaucrats at heart, they liked to do the taxing in a tidy and orderly way. Thus the Roman governor had decreed that all heads of households should return to their home towns to register for taxation purposes.

Bethlehem was an odd sort of place. Even to a people with a long history, as the Jews were, Bethlehem was old. It had always been there, a triangle of stone houses on a limestone hill six miles from Jerusalem. An even more ancient people had named it Ephrata. The Jews, pouring into their promised land, called it Bethlehem, "the house of bread," probably because of the richness of the cornfields below the town. There was always bread in Bethlehem.

Somehow, the town seemed to go to the very roots of the Jewish people. It was strong on its limestone hill, dominating a main road and a wide plain. It was rich in its cornfields and in the flocks grazing on the surrounding hills. David, the mightiest of Jewish kings, had come from Bethlehem; and Ruth, the embodiment of selfless devotion and one of the best-loved women in the long history of the Jews, had lived there. Yet the town had remained small and simple while only six miles away Jerusalem grew in worldly splendor.

Normally Bethlehem was a quiet place. It was far enough from Jerusalem to feel few of the ripples emanating from Herod's court, and, at the same time, too near to be a stopover for travelers on their way to the capital. But now, as a census point for the Romans, Bethlehem was crowded and noisy. Small as it was, it cannot have had much of an inn; what little accommodation was available had doubtless been preempted by the census officials even before the families of the house of David had begun to arrive from all over the country. . . .

Almost certainly, the stable that Mary and Joseph found would not have been a building, not even the primitive wood and thatch structure familiar in religious art. More likely, it was one of the limestone caves common to the area. It would have been warm and dry and probably, by the standards of the day, even clean. Far from feeling abandoned and unwanted, Joseph and Mary must have been both relieved and grateful for its shelter. Time might have decreed that Mary would have to give birth to the child by the roadside. But, by the grace of God, they had reached Bethlehem and had found shelter. And so it was here, according to Luke, in a cave stable, in a small, crowded, noisy town, that the most momentous birth in history took place.

Then
be ye glad,
good
people,
This night
for all
the year,
And light ye
up your
candles,
For His star
it shineth
clear.

—Old English
Carol

And,

behold, thou shalt conceive in thy womb, and bring forth a son, and shalt call his name JESUS. He shall be great, and shall be called the Son of the Highest:

THE PEACEFUL NIGHT

John Milton

But peaceful was the night
Wherein the Prince of light
    His reign of peace upon the earth began:
The winds, with wonder whist,
Smoothly the waters kist,
    Whispering new joys to the mild Ocean,
Who now hath quite forgot to rave,
While birds of calm sit brooding on the charmed wave.

The stars, with deep amaze,
Stand fixed in steadfast gaze,
    Bending one way their precious influence,
And will not take their flight,
For all the morning light,
    Or Lucifer, that often warned them thence;
But in their glimmering orbs did glow
Until their Lord Himself bespake, and bade them go.

And though the shady gloom
Had given day her room,
    The sun himself withheld his wonted speed,
And hid his head for shame,
As his inferior flame
    The new enlightened world no more should need;
He saw a greater sun appear
Than his bright throne or burning axletree could bear.

Opposite: *The Adoration of the Shepherds*, Peter Paul Rubens, 1577–1640.

And the
Lord
God shall
give unto him
the throne of
his father
David:
And he shall
reign over
the house
of Jacob
for ever;
and of his
kingdom
there shall be
no end.

—Luke 1:31–33

For
unto us a
child
is born,
unto us a
son
is given:
and the
government
shall be
upon
his
shoulder:

The Nativity, Gerrit Van
Honthorst, 1590–1656.

And
his
name
shall be called
Wonderful,
Counsellor,
The mighty
God,
The
everlasting
Father, The
Prince
of Peace.

—Isaiah 9:6

The first
Noel
the Angel
did say,
Was to
certain
poor
shepherds
in fields
as they lay:

THE CHRISTMAS STORY

Luke 2:6–20

And so it was, that, while they were there, the days were accomplished that she should be delivered. And she brought forth her firstborn son, and wrapped him in swaddling clothes, and laid him in a manger; because there was no room for them in the inn.

And there were in the same country shepherds abiding in the field, keeping watch over their flock by night. And, lo, the angel of the Lord came upon them, and the glory of the Lord shone round about them: and they were sore afraid.

And the angel said unto them, Fear not: for, behold, I bring you good tidings of great joy, which shall be to all people. For unto you is born this day in the city of David a Saviour, which is Christ the Lord. And this shall be a sign unto you; Ye shall find the babe wrapped in swaddling clothes, lying in a manger.

And suddenly there was with the angel a multitude of the heavenly host praising God, and saying, Glory to God in the highest, and on earth peace, good will toward men.

And it came to pass, as the angels were gone away from them into heaven, the shepherds said one to another, Let us now go even unto Bethlehem, and see this thing which is come to pass, which the Lord hath made known unto us. And they came with haste, and found Mary, and Joseph, and the babe lying in a manger.

And when they had seen it, they made known abroad the saying which was told them concerning this child. And all they that heard it wondered at those things which were told them by the shepherds.

But Mary kept all these things, and pondered them in her heart. And the shepherds returned, glorifying and praising God for all the things that they had heard and seen, as it was told unto them.

In
fields
where
they lay
keeping
their
sheep
On a cold
winter's
night
that was
so deep.

—Old Carol

Opposite: *Adoration of the Shepherds*, Guido Reni, 1575–1642.

He took the young child and his mother by night, and departed into Egypt . . . that it might be fulfilled which was spoken of the Lord by the prophet, saying Out of Egypt have I called my son.

—Matthew 2:14, 15

Opposite: *Flight into Egypt*, Julius Schnorr von Carolsfeld, 1749–1872.

LEGEND OF THE FLIGHT INTO EGYPT

Vera E. Walker

Long, long ago, on the dark and sorrowful night when Herod had made up his mind to kill the Child born to be King, His father and mother stole out of Bethlehem and made their way towards the far-off land of Egypt for safety. The light of Joseph's lantern made strange shadows flicker along the narrow street as he led the little ass forward, and Mary drew her cloak closer round the babe as if to shield Him from evil. They went quickly, lest Herod's spies should be at work even now, yet not as if in fear. They went along the ridges of the stony hills first, and then climbed down into the plains and turned their faces towards the blue sea and the desert country that lies between Palestine and Egypt, choosing paths which travellers rarely followed. It was in these lonely places, full of dangers, that many strange and beautiful things took place. . . .

They travelled by night mostly, for the day was too hot for walking, and as they went the wild creatures of the desert came out of their dens in search of food. The little grey jackals moved like swift shadows about them; the desert birds circled around their heads; lions roared in the distance. Yet all seemed friendly. The jackals would trot by their side without snarling; the lions walked with them as a bodyguard; the birds flew peacefully overhead. In the presence of the Babe of Bethlehem the creatures were at peace with one another and did no harm. . . .

Near Egypt they came to a dark place leading through a wood, and as they went a band of robbers rushed out to meet them. They were fierce, rough men, who thought nothing of killing an old man for the sake of his ass or the few goods he carried with him. But, as the young chief came forward he saw the babe smiling in His mother's arms, and he gave an order that checked his men, and spoke kindly to the travellers. Still looking at the babe he led them into his cave and begged them to rest there till morning. The robber's wife brought them cakes and honey and fruit, and they lay down peacefully to sleep. Next morning . . . the chief entered and taking them outside, showed them a good road which would take them where they wished to go. "Farewell," he said to them as they rode away, "and in whatever place you are remember me who have lodged you this night."

So the travellers passed on, and came quickly to the land of Egypt, where they lived safely till news of Herod's death reached them. For God is Lord of all creatures, of the wild beasts and the hearts of men, and He would let no harm come to His child.

ABOUT THE BEGINNINGS OF CHRISTMAS

Isaiah's prophecies of the coming Messiah were so accurate that his book has been called, by some, the "fifth Gospel."

The Biblical meaning of the word MESSIAH is an individual sent by God to change the course of history and save the people from suffering. The word comes from a Hebrew word meaning "anointed." Its Greek translation is CHRISTOS.

Jesus descended from David, who was himself a shepherd from Bethlehem. The shepherds present at the nativity symbolized the description of Jesus, who would call Himself the "Good Shepherd," knowing that all in Palestine would understand the love and care a shepherd shows for his sheep.

Since the time of David, there had been an inn, called a caravansary, near Bethlehem because the town was on the main route between Jerusalem and Egypt.

Provincial governors of the Roman Empire were empowered to conduct a census in order to organize Rome's tax rolls. It was such a mandate that sent Joseph and Mary on a ninety-mile journey to Bethlehem.

How wonderfully acted Divine Providence, that on the day the sun was born—Christ should be born.

—ST. CYPRIAN,
THIRD CENTURY

We hold this day holy, not like the pagans because of the birth of the sun, but because of Him who made it.

—ST. AUGUSTINE,
FOURTH CENTURY

POSADOS is a Mexican tradition commemorating Mary and Joseph's journey into Bethlehem. Each night for nine nights, Christians carry figures of the holy couple through the streets of their villages. When they reach the sight chosen as the "inn," the innkeeper asks who the travelers are and what they seek. When they reveal their meager request, this innkeeper, unlike the ancient innkeeper of Bethlehem, welcomes the couple to enter and find comfort. On the final night of the procession, Christmas Eve, the people carry a figure of the Christ Child with them.

A manger was a feeding trough for domestic animals. Whether the manger spoken of in the Bible was in a cave or a stable or the courtyard is not known. Tradition says the birth took place in one of the many habitable caves in the hills around Bethlehem which were often used to stable the animals.

The use of the term XMAS dates back to the eleventh or twelfth century and derives from the use of the Greek letter CHI, which resembles the letter X. To the Greeks, Chi is a symbol of Christ, and in their language it is the first letter in the word CHRIST.

On the eighth day, the Christ Child was circumcised and given what was then a common name: the Greek name JESUS—YESHUA or JOSHUA in Hebrew— which meant "Yahweh is salvation."

Mary, the mother of Jesus, was the child of Joachim and Anne, Jews who lived in either Jerusalem or Galilee. Mary spent her childhood in Nazareth and was likely espoused to Joseph at the age of fourteen, as was tradition for girls of her day. Some Biblical scholars believe that Mary and Joseph had children together after the birth of Jesus.

Joseph was a Nazareth carpenter and a descendant of King David. After Joseph and Mary brought Jesus to the Temple at the age of twelve, Joseph did not again appear in the Biblical accounts of Jesus' life.

Jewish babies were traditionally cleansed with water and then their bodies rubbed with salt to prevent infection. They were then swaddled; long linen strips were tightly wound around the infant's body, preventing him from excessively moving his arms and legs and ensuring that he would grow straight and strong. Swaddling continued for at least the first six months of life.

CHRISTMAS DAY

In pre-Christian times, the birth of the "Unconquered Sun" was the most important festival of the Roman Empire. In adapting some of the practices of non-Christian festivals, the early Christian church captured the spirit of the festival, which was rebirth, and transformed it to signify the coming of Christ. Thus, Christmas now celebrates the birth of the unconquered *Son*.

In all Christendom, Christmas remains the most festive holiday of all the year. But it has not always been so. The history of the day owes much to those secular winter celebrations. Christmas past has ranged from lavish celebrations to actual bans on any observance at all. Added to this mix of sacred and secular, celebrations and bans, were charming and unique customs from many cultures, all of which contributed much to what is now the rich tradition of Christmas Day.

Photograph: A lake south of Munich, Germany.

Rise, happy morn; rise, holy morn; Draw forth the cheerful day from night: O Father, touch the east, and light the light that shone when Hope was born.
—Alfred, Lord Tennyson

Christmas

is coming,

the

geese

are getting

fat,

Please to put

a penny

in the

old man's

hat;

Good King Wenceslas

Translated by J. M. Neale

Good King Wenceslas looked out
    On the Feast of Stephen;
When the snow lay round about,
    Deep, and crisp, and even:
Brightly shone the moon that night,
    Though the frost was cruel,
When a poor man came in sight,
    Gath'ring winter fuel.

"Hither, page, and stand by me,
    If thou knowest it, telling,
Yonder peasant, who is he?
    Where and what his dwelling?"
"Sire, he lives a good league hence,
    Underneath the mountain;
Right against the forest fence,
    By Saint Agnes' fountain."

"Bring me flesh, and bring me wine,
    Bring me pine-logs hither:
Thou and I will see him dine,
    When we bear them thither."
Page and monarch forth they went,
    Forth they went together;
Through the rude wind's wild lament
    And the bitter weather. . . .

In his master's steps he trod,
    Where the snow lay dinted;
Heat was in the very sod
    Which the saint had printed.
Therefore, Christian men, be sure,
    Wealth or rank possessing,
Ye who now will bless the poor,
    Shall yourselves find blessing.

Opposite: *Frozen Out*, George
Dunlop Leslie, 1835–1921.

If you haven't got
a penny,
a ha'penny
will do,
If you
haven't
got a
ha'penny,
God bless
you.

—Old English
Rhyme

I
  sing
    the birth
      was born
        to-night,
          The
          Author
            both of
            life and
          light,

            Angels
              so did
                sound it;

A Day for Christmas

The Gospel stories of Jesus' birth do not reveal to us the year or the date of His nativity. Biblical scholars have long agreed, however, that there is enough factual evidence to place Jesus' birthday in the year 6 B.C. We are told that Jesus was born during the reign of Herod the Great, and it is known that Herod's reign ended with his death in 4 B.C. Just before he died, Herod ordered all male children under the age of two be executed. His order, issued out of fear, was meant to rid the world of the boy being hailed as the new King of the Jews. Jesus, if He were born in 6 B.C., would have been approaching the age of two when Herod's violent decree was issued.

For more than three centuries, as Christianity spread slowly throughout the world, Christians remembered and celebrated the birth of Christ on different days and in different fashions; it was not until the Roman Emperor Constantine converted to Christianity that December 25 became the official Christmas Day. Constantine had been an adherent of a Persian religion called Mithraism, which had taken root in Roman culture in the third century A.D. On December 25th, Mithraists celebrated the festival of *Dies Invicti Solis*, or the Day of the Invincible Sun, in honor of Mithra, who was said to have been born on this date. When Constantine declared himself a believer in Jesus Christ, he left Mithra behind, but he decreed the official Roman day of celebration of the birthday of Jesus Christ to be December 25, the same day as the celebration of Mithra. This was also the season of the Roman holiday of Saturnalia and of the Kalends of January, two highly spirited celebrations marked by great feasting and revelry. In those days, Christianity grew in a world full of mythology, superstition, and competing gods; and Constantine understood that the best means of winning converts was not by forbidding the old celebrations, but by turning old traditions to the new Christian purpose.

One element almost all pre-Christian cultures and religions shared was the winter solstice celebration—rituals and festivals meant to help the people through the darkest, shortest days of the year and hasten the return of spring. Christmas Day became the new center of the winter solstice, and Jesus Christ the new light in the darkest time of year. In 350 A.D., Pope Julius I decreed December 25 as the official Christian celebration day for the birth of Jesus. Two centuries later, Roman Emperor Justinian gave further permanence to the date by declaring it a civil holiday on which all work must cease. Jesus Christ may not have been born on December 25, but more than fifteen hundred years have proven that there is no more wonderful time to celebrate His arrival.

And like the ravished shepherds said, Who saw the light, and were afraid, Yet searched, and true they found it.

The Son of God, th'eternal King, That did us all salvation bring, And freed the soul from danger,

Opposite: *A Winter's Afternoon, Scene near Wotton, Surrey,* Edward Wilkins Waite, 1854–1924.

ENGLAND'S GREAT CHRISTMAS

Maymie Richardson Krythe

In England—so the story goes—Christmas was first observed as a holiday in A.D. 521, when King Arthur celebrated a warrior's victory. Many guests sat at his famous Round Table and enjoyed a bounteous meal. They were entertained by wandering minstrels, who sang of the mighty deeds of their national heroes. Jugglers, harpists, and pipe players added to the enjoyment; also such pastimes as gambling, playing dice or backgammon, along with hunting, hawking, and jousting, were popular when the Anglo-Saxons got together for their winter celebrations. . . .

During the ninth century, seven petty kingdoms in Britain were unified under Alfred the Great, the model for King Arthur, who annually set aside twelve days for Yule festivities. In 878, while he and his court were feasting in lavish style, their enemies, the Danes, suddenly rode through the land of the West Saxons and made a surprise attack. Alfred's army was scattered; and the king, with a small band, fled to the forest. According to one account, Alfred, in order to discover the Danish strength, disguised himself as a Christmas minstrel. He spent several days in their camp, where he pleased them with his ability as an entertainer, and left without their learning his identity.

After the Normans had conquered England in 1066, they built great castles and introduced their feudal system with its strict division of people into various classes, from the king and his luxury-loving nobles, down to the meanest serf. Christmas became gayer than ever before; each great lord kept open house; and food and drink were given to all who entered his walls during the holy season. This entertaining and revelry continued until Twelfth Night, January 6.

In the spacious manor halls, great fires blazed on wide hearths, lighting the walls, high ceilings, and decoration of holiday greenery. The "Lord of Misrule," a person who was well-paid for his services, presided over his subjects during the Yule period with absolute power. He planned the entertainment with the assistance of jesters, mummers, and musicians, who played on their bagpipes, harps, drums, fiddles, or flageolets. Games, such as snapdragon, dancing, and caroling, were the order of the time.

During the Middle Ages, Christmas was England's most popular holiday with everyone, from the king to the beggars, taking part. All who could do so quit work and gave themselves entirely to pleasure. And no people entered more heartily into the joys of the Yule season than the Britons.

He
whom the
whole
world
could not
take, The
Word,
which
heaven
and earth
did make,
Was now
laid
in a
manger.

A Day for Celebration and Contemplation

The festival of the KALENDS is celebrated everywhere as far as the limits of the Roman empire extend. . . . Luxurious abundance is found in the houses of the rich, but also in the house of the poor; better food than usual is put upon the table. The impulse to spend seizes everyone. He who erstwhile was accustomed and preferred to live poorly now enjoys himself as much as his means will allow. . . .

—LIBANIUS, FOURTH-CENTURY GREEK HISTORIAN

The English Christmas of the late Middle Ages was a time of indulgence and extravagance. The King of France gave a Christmas gift of a live elephant to England's King Henry III. There was also an excess in Christmas feasting. Henry III once ordered six hundred oxen slaughtered for royal Christmas feasting. The season was also marked by pageants and plays and musical productions.

In ancient times, the Northern people worshiped the sun as the giver of life and light. Their festivals in its honor took place near the shortest day of the year when the sun seemed to stand still for twelve days before it began its upward climb, which resulted in spring and the coming of new life to the world. In the North, the sun was thought of as a wheel which was known as "hweol," and it is perhaps from this word that the term Yule was derived.

Among the Romans, the SATURNALIA holiday lasted from December seventeenth to December twenty-fourth. Another holiday was KALENDS, on January first, which marked the beginning of the new year. Both of these holidays were celebrated with feasting, great merriment, the decorating of homes, and the giving of gifts.

England continued its grand tradition of Christmas throughout the Middle Ages and through the reign of the Stuart kings. With the Protestant Reformation of the sixteenth century, however, the English Christmas was transformed. The Calvinists saw Christmas as a secular celebration which was an excuse for excess and unruly behavior.

For preventing disorders arising in several places within this jurisdiction, by reason of some still observing such festivals as were superstitiously kept in other countries, to the great dishonor of God and offense of others, it is therefore ordered by this court and the authority thereof, that whosoever shall be found observing any such day as Christmas or the like, either by forebearing of labor, feasting, or any other way, upon any such accounts as foresaid, every such person so offending shall pay for every such offense five shillings, as a fine to the county.

—MASSACHUSETTS BAY COLONY DECREE OF MAY 11, 1659

After Puritan Oliver Cromwell came to power in 1642, the British parliament passed a law forbidding Christmas celebrations. Workplaces were to continue with business as usual. Candles, decorations, even Christmas cakes were included in the ban. Town criers walked the streets to announce the ban, crying "No Christmas!" throughout the whole of England.

Armenian Christians have never accepted December 25 as the birthday of Christ, and instead continue to celebrate the nativity on January 6, or Epiphany. Their celebration includes a week-long fast leading up to a complete fast on Christmas Eve. After church services on the night before Christmas, Armenians traditionally return home for a holiday dinner and family caroling.

Puritan rule lasted less than twenty years in England. With the Restoration of the monarchy, Christmas again was legal. But never again would Christmas in England, or Christmas anywhere, reach the extremes of secular celebration it had known during the British Middle Ages.

In the U.S., the first state to legalize Christmas as a holiday was Alabama in 1836, the last was Oklahoma (Indian Territory) in 1890. Most states had done so by 1880.

ENGRAVING BY RANDOLPH CALDECOTT, FROM THE SKETCH BOOK.

What
comfort
by him
do we
win,
Who made
himself
the price
of sin,
To make
us
heirs of
glory!

CHRISTMAS IN PLYMOUTH
William Bradford

December 25, 1620. On the day called Christmas-day, the Gov'r called them out to work (as was usual), but the most of this new company excused themselves, and said it went against their consciences to work on the day. So the Gov'r told them that if they made it a matter of conscience, he would spare them until they were better informed. So he led away the rest, and left them: but when they came home at noon from their work, he found them in the street at play, openly; some pitching the ball, and some at stoole ball, and such like sports. So he went to them and took away their implements, and told them it was against his conscience that they should play and others work. If they made the keeping of it a matter of devotion, let them keep their houses, but there should be no gaming or reveling in the streets. Since which time nothing hath been attempted that way, at least, openly.

MAKE WE MERRY
from *Balliol Manuscript* of about 1540

Let no man come into this hall,
Groom, page, nor yet marshall,
But that some sport he bring withal!
For now is the time of Christmas!

If that he say, he cannot sing,
Some other sport then let him bring!
That it may please at this feasting!
For now is the time of Christmas!

If he say he can naught do,
Then for my love ask him no mo!
But to the stocks then let him go!
For now is the time of Christmas.

Photograph opposite: Yosemite
National Park, California.

To
see this
Babe,
all innocence,
A martyr
born in our
defence,
Can man
forget the
story?

—Ben Jonson

May each
be found thus
as the
year
circles round,
With mirth
and good
humor
each
Christmas
be crowned,
And may all
who have
plenty
of riches
in store

With their
bountiful
blessings
make
happy
the poor,
For never as yet
was it counted
a crime
To be
merry
and cheery
at that
happy time.

—Author
Unknown

*Salisbury in Winter: Coach Arrives at
the Star Inn*, John Charles Maggs,
1819–1895.

CHARLES DICKENS AND THE SPIRIT OF CHRISTMAS

Joy to the world! the Lord is come: Let earth receive her King; Let ev'ry heart prepare Him room, And heav'n and nature sing.

Charles Dickens was a writer of unparalleled popularity in England during his day. A series of novels, *The Pickwick Papers*, *Nicholas Nickleby*, *Oliver Twist*, *The Old Curiosity Shop*, and *Barnaby Rudge*, had made him perhaps the most cherished and widely read author Great Britain had ever

American Homestead Winter,
Currier and Ives, 1857–1907.

known. But in October 1843, as he traveled to the city of Manchester to speak on behalf of the country's poor working class, he was in a blue mood. Not only had his despair over the plight of the poor begun to distract him from his work, but his most recent project, a serial novel called *Martin Chuzzlewit*, was not progressing well. The public showed little interest, and Dickens himself could not find motivation to go on with the project. But as he walked the streets of Manchester one night that autumn, he was struck by an inspiration. Dickens had always treasured the Christmas season, and he had tried through his writing to keep the old spirit of Christmas alive in his country where so many were struggling to feed their families and had little time or money to spend on Christmas, and where so many others had become so enraptured with their own excesses of money that they had little inclination to open their hearts at Christmastime, or any time, to help those less fortunate. Dickens left Manchester with a story in mind, a story that revived his enthusiasm for writing and began to lift his spirits. Little did he know that this story would become a permanent source of Christmas inspiration to people across the world.

Dickens called his story *A Christmas Carol*. He made certain that it was published at low cost and that it was sold at a price affordable to all who wished to buy it, thus ensuring that he would never make much money from the story. But Dickens succeeded beyond his wildest dreams in reaching the hearts and minds of readers with his charming Christmas tale. Few Christmas stories have been as widely read or warmly embraced. Dickens's characters are unforgettable; from the miserly Scrooge to the kind-hearted Bob Cratchit to the innocent Tiny Tim, each has become a part of Christmas everywhere the holiday is celebrated. In his lifetime, Dickens often spoke of what he liked to call the "carol philosophy" of Christmas. In his mind, this was "a good time, a kind, forgiving, charitable, pleasant time: the only time I know of, in the long calendar of the year, when men and women seem by one consent to open their shut-up hearts freely, and to think of other people below them as if they really were fellow-passengers to the grave, and not another race of creatures bound on other journeys." Nothing so eloquently embodies this philosophy as does *A Christmas Carol*.

A British legend tells that on the day Dickens died a poor young girl heard the news and asked her mother with great sadness if this could really be true. "Yes," her mother quietly told her, Mr. Dickens was gone. "Shall Father Christmas die too?" the girl is said to have asked.

Joy
to the earth!
the Saviour
reigns;
Let men
their songs
employ;
While fields
and floods,
rocks, hills
and plains,
Repeat
the sounding
joy.

THE SPIRIT OF CHRISTMAS

Charles Dickens

No

more let sins

and sorrows

grow,

Nor thorns

infest the

ground;

He comes to

make His

blessings

flow

Far as the

curse is

found.

And numerous indeed are the hearts to which Christmas brings a brief season of happiness and enjoyment. How many families whose members have been dispersed and scattered far and wide, in the restless struggles of life, are then re-united, and meet once again in that happy state of companionship and mutual good-will, which is a source of such pure and unalloyed delight, . . . How many old recollections, and how many dormant sympathies, does Christmas time awaken!

We write these words now, many miles distant from the spot at which, year after year, we met on that day, a merry and joyous circle. Many of the hearts that throb so gaily then, have ceased to beat; many of the looks that shone so brightly then, have ceased to glow; the hands we grasped, have grown cold; the eyes we sought, have hid their lustre in the grave; and yet the old house, the room, the merry voices and smiling faces, the jest, the laugh, the most minute and trivial circumstance connected with those happy meetings, crowd upon our mind at each recurrence of the season, as if the last assemblage had been but yesterday. Happy, happy Christmas, that can win us back to the delusions of our childish days, that can recall to the old man the pleasures of his youth, and transport the sailor and the traveller, thousands of miles away, back to his own fireside and his quiet home!

Winter—Image for the Month of December, 1841.

HOME FOR CHRISTMAS

Elizabeth Bowen

This is meeting time again. Home is the magnet. The winter land roars and hums with the eager speed of return journeys. The dark is noisy and bright with late-night arrivals—doors thrown open, running shadows on snow, open arms, kisses, voices and laughter, laughter at everything and nothing. Inarticulate, giddying and confused are those original minutes of being back again. The very familiarity of everything acts like a shock. Contentment has to be drawn in slowly, steadyingly, in deep breaths—there is so much of it. We rely on home not to change, and it does not, wherefore we give thanks. Again Christmas: abiding point of return. Set apart by its mystery, mood and magic, the season seems in a way to stand outside time. All that is dear, that is lasting, renews its hold on us: we are home again. . . .

This glow of Christmas, has it not in it also the gold of a harvest? "They shall return with joy, bringing their sheaves with them." To the festival, to each other, we bring in wealth. More to tell, more to understand, more to share. Each we have garnered in yet another year; to be glad, to celebrate to the full, we are come together. How akin we are to each other, how speechlessly dear and one in the fundamentals of being, Christmas shows us. No other time grants us, quite, this vision—round the tree or gathered before the fire we perceive anew, with joy, one another's faces. And each time faces come to mean more.

Is it not one of the mysteries of life that life should, after all, be so simple? Yes, as simple as Christmas, simple as this. Journeys through the dark to a lighted door, arms open. Laughter-smothered kisses, kiss-smothered laughter. And blessedness in the heart of it all. Here are the verities, all made gay with tinsel! Dear, silly Christmas-card saying and cracker mottoes—let them speak! Or, since still we cannot speak, let us sing! Dearer than memory, brighter than expectation is the ever returning *now* of Christmas. Why else, each time we greet its return, should happiness ring out in us like a peal of bells?

He
rules the world
with truth and
grace;
And makes
the nations
prove
The glories
of His
righteousness,
And
wonders
of His
Love.

—Isaac Watts

CHRISTMAS IN THE OLDEN TIME

Sir Walter Scott

On Christmas Eve the bells were rung;
The damsel donned her kirtle sheen;
The hall was dressed with holly green;
Forth to the wood did merry men go,
To gather in the mistletoe.
Thus opened wide the baron's hall
To vassal, tenant, serf and all;
Power laid his rod of rule aside
And ceremony doffed his pride.
The heir, with roses in his shoes,
That night might village partner choose;
The lord, underogating, share
The vulgar game of "Post and Pair."
All hailed, with uncontrolled delight,
And general voice, the happy night
That to the cottage, as the crown,
Brought tidings of salvation down.
The fire, with well-dried logs supplied,
Went roaring up the chimney wide;
The huge hall-table's oaken face,
Scrubbed till it shone, the day to grace,
Bore then upon its massive board
No mark to part the squire and lord.
Then was brought in the lusty brawn
By old blue-coated serving man;
Then the grim boar's head frowned on high,
Crested with bays and rosemary.

Well can the green-garbed ranger tell
How, when and where the monster fell;
What dogs before his death he tore,
And all the baitings of the boar.
The wassail round, in good brown bowls,
Garnished with ribbons, blithely trowls.
There the huge sirloin reeked: hard by
Plum-porridge stood, and Christmas pie;
Nor failed old Scotland to produce,
At such high-tide, her savory goose.
Then came the merry maskers in,
And carols roared with blithesome din.
If unmelodious was the song,
It was a hearty note, and strong;
Who lists may in their murmuring see
Traces of ancient mystery;
White shirts supplied the masquerade,
And smutted cheeks the visors made;
But O, what maskers richly dight,
Can boast of bosoms half so light!
England was "merry England" when
Old Christmas brought his sports again;
'Twas Christmas broached the mightiest ale,
'Twas Christmas told the merriest tale;
A Christmas gambol oft would cheer
The poor man's heart through half the year.

CHRISTMAS TRADITIONS

Washington Irving

O f all the old festivals . . . that of Christmas awakens the strongest and most heartfelt associations. There is a tone of solemn and sacred feeling that blends with our conviviality, and lifts the spirit to a state of hallowed and elevated enjoyment. The services of the church about this season are extremely tender and inspiring; they dwell on the beautiful story of the origin of our faith, and the pastoral scenes that accompanied its announcement; they gradually increase in fervor and pathos during the season of Advent, until they break forth in full jubilee on the morning that brought peace and good-will to men. I do not know a grander effect of music on the moral feelings than to hear the full choir and the pealing organ performing a Christmas anthem in a cathedral, and filling every part of the vast pile with triumphant harmony.

It is a beautiful arrangement, also, derived from the days of yore, that this festival, which commemorates the announcement of the religion of peace and love, has been made the season for gathering together of family connections, and drawing closer again those bands of kindred hearts, which the cares and pleasures and sorrows of the world are continually operating to cast loose; of calling back the children of a family, who have launched forth in life, and wandered widely asunder, once more to assemble the paternal hearth, that rallying-place of the affections, there to grow young and loving again among the endearing mementoes of childhood.

There is something in the very season of the year, that gives a charm to the festivity of Christmas. At other times, we derive a great portion of our pleasures from the mere beauties of Nature. Our feelings sally forth and dissipate themselves over the sunny landscape, and we "live abroad and everywhere." . . . But in the depth of winter, when Nature lies despoiled of every charm and wrapped in her shroud of sheeted snow, we turn for our gratifications to moral sources. . . . Our thoughts are more concentrated; our friendly sympathies more aroused. We feel more sensibly the charm of each other's society, and are brought more closely together by dependence on each other for enjoyment. Heart calleth unto heart, and we draw pleasures from the deep wells of living kindness which lie in the quiet recesses of our bosoms. . . . He who can turn churlishly away from contemplating the felicity of his fellow-beings, and can sit down darkling and repining in his loneliness when all around is joyful, may have his moments of strong excitement and selfish gratification, but he wants the genial and social sympathies which constitute the charm of a merry Christmas.

Sing
we all
merrily
Christmas
is here,
The day that
we love
best
Of days in the
year.

—Author Unknown

Opposite: *Snowballing*,
Cornelius Kimmel, 1804–1877.

CHRISTMAS
DECORATIONS

From ancient times, people looked to festive decorations to chase away midwinter darkness, and Christmas provides the perfect opportunity to "deck the halls" with joy as well as holly. Each of our traditional decorations has a special meaning, some originating from secular celebrations, but all now rich with two thousand years of meaning. From poinsettias to mistletoe, from manger scenes to the ubiquitous Christmas tree, our traditional decorations continue to lift our spirits and remind us of the deeply spiritual significance of Christmas.

Photograph: Elmau, Germany.

Let every hall have
boughs of green,
With berries growing
in between,
In the week when
Christmas comes.
—Eleanor Farjeon

The
holly and
the ivy,
Now they
are full well
grown,
Of all the
trees that are
in the
wood,
The holly
bears the
crown.

CHRISTMAS GREENERY

Long before the Christian era, evergreens held a special place in folklore and legend as symbols of life and renewal. In the darkest, coldest days of winter, the vibrant greenery of these plants defied death and served as a reminder of the springtime that would surely come. The many varieties of evergreens, thus, were a perfect fit with the Christmas celebrations that slowly replaced the winter solstice festivities of many cultures. Christmas is, after all, a celebration of new life and of the promise of eternal life, and evergreens have been a part of the holiday from the very start.

Two of the evergreens with ancient legends attached to them are the holly and the ivy. Their symbolism is twofold, for not only do they retain their greenery through the winter, but they also bear fruit during this dark, cold season. Ancient tradition saw holly as masculine and ivy as feminine and required that homes be decorated with both at year's end to promise full blessings on the family in the months to come. Early Christians brought holly and ivy into their homes fashioned into wreaths. The holly in particular came to symbolize the crown of thorns worn by Jesus at his crucifixion, with the plants' bright red berries symbolic of His blood.

Mistletoe is another evergreen that has become synonymous with Christmastime but which traces its roots back to ancient legend. Pre-Christian cultures regarded mistletoe as sacred and assigned to it the power to give life, to cure disease, and to neutralize poisons. The Celtic Druids hung the plant in doorways where adversaries would come to reconcile, forgive wrongs, and renew friendships. Very likely, this practice is the root of the modern tradition of kissing under the mistletoe at Christmastime. In Christian legend, mistletoe was once a stately tree, but because it provided the wood for the cross upon which Christ was crucified, the tree was reduced forever after to a parasitic plant.

The most significant of all Christmas evergreens is the fir tree, and many legends exist about its origins as a symbol for Christmas. In medieval times, in the days leading up to Christmas, Christians performed dramas reenacting man's fall from grace in the Garden of Eden. The Garden was symbolized by a single fir tree hung with bright red apples. Eventually, the dramas fell out of style, but the trees remained. The apples, originally symbolic of man's fall, were joined by wafers, a traditional symbol of man's salvation. Through the ages, apples and wafers evolved into the brightly colored ornaments and decorated cookies that we see on Christmas trees today. Fir trees, like the holly, ivy, and mistletoe, have proven themselves to be eternal symbols of Christmas. They will forever brighten our homes and turn our thoughts toward the celebration of life and hope and renewal.

The
holly bears a
blossom,
As white
as the lily
flower,
And Mary
bore sweet
Jesus Christ
To be
our sweet
Saviour.

—Medieval
English Carol

Photograph: Multnomah
County, Oregon.

CHRISTMAS EVE AT MR. WARDLE'S

From *The Pickwick Papers*
Charles Dickens

'Tis merry 'neath the mistletoe, When holly berries glisten bright; When Christmas fires gleam and glow,

From the center of the ceiling of this kitchen, old Wardle had just suspended with his own hands a huge branch of mistletoe, and this same branch of mistletoe instantaneously gave rise to a scene of general and most delightful struggling and confusion; in the midst of which Mr. Pickwick with a gallantry which would have done honour to a descendant of Lady Trollimglower herself, took the old lady by the hand, led her beneath the mystic branch, and saluted her in all courtesy and decorum. The old lady submitted to this piece of practical politeness with all the dignity which befitted so important and serious a solemnity, but the younger ladies not being so thoroughly imbued with a superstitious veneration of the custom, or imagining that the value of a salute is very much enhanced if it cost a little trouble to obtain it, screamed and struggled, and ran into corners, and threatened and remonstrated, and did everything but leave the room, until some of the less adventurous gentlemen were on the point of desisting, when they all at once found it useless to resist any longer, and submitted to be kissed with a good grace. Mr. Winkle kissed the young lady with the black eyes, and Mr. Snodgrass kissed Emily; and Mr. Weller, not being particular about the form of being under the mistletoe, kissed Emma and the other female servants, just as he caught them. As to the poor relations, they kissed everybody, not even excepting the plainer portion of the young-lady visitors, who, in their excessive confusion, ran right under the mistletoe, directly it was hung up, without knowing it! Wardle stood with his back to the fire, surveying the whole scene, with the utmost satisfaction.

Opposite: *Mr. Fezziwig's Ball*, from the frontispiece of *A Christmas Carol*, Artist Unknown.

When
wintry winds
so wildly blow,
And all the
meadows
round are
white—
'Tis
merry
'neath the
mistletoe!

A
privilege
'tis then,
you know,
To exercise
time-honored
rite;
When
Christmas
fires
gleam and
glow,

DECEMBER 26, 1855
Nathaniel Hawthorne

*In 1855, Nathaniel Hawthorne was serving as the American consul in Liverpool,
England, and described the "shocking" custom of kissing under the mistletoe.*

On Christmas Eve, and yesterday, there were little branches of
mistletoe hanging in several parts of our house, in the kitchen, the
entries, the parlor, and the smoking room—suspended from the gas-fit-
tings. The maids of the house did their utmost to entrap the gentlemen
boarders, old and young, under these privileged places, and there to kiss
them, after which they were expected to pay a shilling. It is very queer,
being customarily so respectful, that they should assume this license now,
absolutely trying to pull the gentlemen into the kitchen by main force,
and kissing the harder and more abundantly, the more they were resis-
ted. A little rosy-cheeked Scotch lass—at other times very modest—was
the most active in this business. I doubt whether any gentleman but
myself escaped. I heard old Mr. Smith parleying with the maids last
evening, and pleading his age; but he seems to have met with no mercy;
for there was the sound of prodigious smacking, immediately afterwards.

SONG OF THE HOLLY
William Shakespeare

Blow, blow thou winter wind—
Thou art not so unkind
    As man's ingratitude!
Thy tooth is not so keen,
Because thou art not seen,
    Although thy breath be rude.
Heigh ho! sing heigh ho! unto the green holly:
Most friendship is feigning, most loving mere folly.
    Then heigh ho! the holly!
    This life is most jolly!
Freeze, freeze, thou bitter sky—
Thou dost not bite so nigh
    As benefits forgot!
Though thou the waters warp,
Thy sting is not so sharp
    As friend remembered not.
Heigh ho! sing heigh ho! unto the green holly,
Most friendship is feigning, most loving mere folly.
    Then heigh ho, the holly!
    This life is most jolly!

When
loving lips may
pout, although
With other
lips
they oft
unite—
'Tis
merry
'neath the
mistletoe!

—J. Ashby Sterry

THE HOLLY

Edith King

How happy the holly-tree looks,
and how strong,
Where he stands like a sentinel
all the year long.

Neither dry summer heat
nor cold winter hail
Can make that gay warrior
tremble or quail.

He has beamed all the year,
but bright scarlet he'll glow
When the ground glitters white
with the fresh fallen snow.

But
give me
holly,
bold and jolly,
Honest,
prickly,
shining
holly;

THE CHRISTMAS TREE

John Lewis, Christmas 1875

There [Philadelphia, Pennsylvania] all the people seem to resolve themselves into children for the occasion. The usual arrangement in this country [U.S.] is to have two parlors—be it large or small house—opening to each other by sliding doors, the first being for state occasions. As large and fine a tree as could be accommodated being procured and set up, it is covered with every conceivable shape into which coloured and gilt paper and card can be cut, and little pictures, glass balls, chains, garlands, etc., anything to make a gay and imposing display. This being finished it is placed mostly in the sliding door way, which allows it to be seen two ways. All the light possible is thrown upon it, often by reflectors, the lattice blinds being thrown open and it is thus open to inspection by passersby.

Opposite: Wooded Winter
Landscape, Mortaratsch,
Peder Monsted.

Pluck
me holly
leaf and
berry
For the
day
when I make
merry.

—Christina
Rossetti

Decorating with Greenery

Holly has distinctive, glossy green leaves with thorny tips and deep red berries. Tradition bestowed a holy status on the holly long before the birth of Christ. It is said that it was a holly bush from which God spoke to Moses.

The Della-Robbia style wreath is an evergreen wreath decorated with pine cones and various fruit. The wreath takes its name from an Italian family who, in the fifteenth century, became famous for their carved, elaborate, fruit-decorated wreaths.

The poinsettia is native to Mexico, and a legend of that country says its creation was a miracle. A small boy, too poor to bring a gift for the Christ Child at his local church, prayed for a gift; and what the Mexicans call the "Flower of the Holy Night" miraculously sprang up at his feet.

Dr. Joel Roberts Poinsett, American ambassador to Mexico and amateur botanist, loved the brilliant red plant he saw while in Mexico. Poinsett brought the flower to his home in South Carolina and gave it his name.

Many legends speak of holly and its association with Jesus. One ancient story is that wherever Jesus walked, holly grew out of his footprints; witnessing this miraculous growth, the animals vowed never to disturb the holy plant.

Engraving by Randolph Caldecott, from *The Sketch Book*.

The first decorated community Christmas tree in America began in Pasadena, California, in 1909. The following year, Boston and New York City added their own public trees; today, nearly every community in America boasts a beautiful tree in the town center at Christmastime.

In 1856, American President Franklin Pierce decorated the first indoor White House Christmas tree, beginning a long and cherished national tradition. In 1920, President Warren Harding oversaw the decoration of the first Christmas tree on the White House lawn.

An employee of the New England Telephone Company was first to imagine a Christmas tree with electric lights instead of burning candles. Ralph Morris took a string of tiny bulbs from the telephone switchboard in 1895 and tried them on his tree. The idea was an immediate and widespread success, as families gladly traded in their beautiful but dangerous candles for the safer light of electricity.

Ornaments designed specifically for Christmas trees were first made by German glass blowers in Thuringia around 1880. Their beautiful and lightweight ornaments lightened the heavy load already bearing down on German Christmas trees decorated with fruit, cookies, and candles.

An ancient legend tells that on the night of Christ's birth, three trees stood outside the manger: an olive, a date palm, and a pine tree. In honor of the newborn Babe, the olive tree gave of its ripe olives and the palm a bountiful supply of dates. The pine, however, had nothing to give until the stars in the sky, seeing the tree's plight, descended from the heavens to adorn the evergreen's branches. Baby Jesus was delighted with this very first Christmas tree.

The first Christmas trees in America were decorated by German settlers in Pennsylvania in the late 1700s.

One early connection between trees and Christmas is the legend of Joseph of Arimathea and the Glastonbury thorn. Traditionally, Joseph is believed to have been the one who took Jesus' body from the cross and carried it to the tomb. It is said that later in life, Joseph settled in Glastonbury where, on Christmas Eve, he climbed atop a hill and drove his walking stick into the earth. Miraculously, his staff was suddenly transformed into a beautiful flowering hawthorn tree. Legend tells that this tree blossomed forever after on Christmas Eve.

THE LEGEND OF THE
CHRISTMAS TREE

O Fir-tree
green!
O Fir-tree
green!
Your leaves
are constant
ever,

One charming old story tells of the young Martin Luther and the first Christmas trees. On Christmas Eve, the legend goes, Luther was walking toward his home through the dark forest. As he looked up through the branches of the stately evergreens, he saw the bright lights of a thousand stars sparkling in the night sky.

When he reached his home, Luther, still moved by the beautiful natural scene he had witnessed, tried to describe it to his family but found that words were inadequate to the task. In a moment of inspiration, Luther is said to have run outside, cut down a tiny fir tree, and carried it into the house, where he placed burning candles on its branches. This, he told his family—the sparkling of lights through the dark green boughs—was what had so moved him in the forest that night.

Whether this story is fact, pure legend, or a mixture of the two, the Christmas tree does seem to have been born in Luther's native Germany. Records from the city of Strasburg reveal that in the year 1605 residents brought evergreens into their home and decorated them with colored paper flowers, apples, cookies, and more. Germany's Christmas celebrations soon centered around the family Christmas tree; and the marketplaces were filled with trees of all sizes and prices, so even the poorest of families could share in the festivities and join around their own tree to sing "O Tannenbaum!"

In Germany, the tree was decorated on Christmas Eve with a star, an angel, sweetmeats, toys, tinsel, nuts, and candles. The custom of decorating a special Christmas tree spread slowly from Germany into Finland, Denmark, Sweden, and Norway. Different cultures developed their own decorations; Lithuanian farmers made windmills from straw; Norwegian fishermen made ornaments from fish net; and the Poles festooned their Christmas trees with feathers, ribbons, and colored paper.

England was introduced to Christmas trees by Prince Albert and Queen Victoria in 1841, the year their first son was born. Albert decided to have a Christmas tree at Windsor castle in honor of the tradition of his native land. It was beautifully decorated, and an angel with outstretched arms rested on the top. The prince is said to have written to his father of the tree's splendor and how much enjoyment it gave him, and the queen spoke of how happy her children were with its festive, ornamented boughs. Many in England soon followed Prince Albert and Queen Victoria's example—their fondness for the Christmas tree

Opposite: *A Joyful Christmas*, Artist Unknown.

inspired families the world over to decorate their own tree for the holiday. This young royal couple, hundreds of years removed from Martin Luther and his midnight walk through the forest, was in many ways responsible for the Christmas tree that is now a central and unchanging part of Christmas tradition in countries throughout the world.

Not
only through
the summer
time,
But through
the winter's
snow
and rime
You're fresh
and green
forever.

O Fir-tree green! O Fir-tree green! I still shall love you dearly! How oft to me on Christmas night Your laden boughs have brought delight.

Photograph: East Lake, New Marlborough, Massachusetts.

VICTORIA AND ALBERT'S CHRISTMAS TREE

From *The Illustrated London News*, 1848

The Christmas tree is annually prepared by her majesty's command for the Royal children. . . . The tree employed for this festive purpose is a young fir of about eight feet high, and has six tiers of branches. On each tier, or branch, are arranged a dozen wax tapers. Pendant from the branches are elegant trays, baskets, bonbonnières, and other receptacles for sweetmeats of the most varied and expensive kind; and of all forms, colours, and degrees of beauty.

Fancy cakes, gilt gingerbread and eggs filled with sweetmeats, are also suspended by variously colored ribbons from the branches. The tree, which stands upon a table covered with white damask, is supported at the root by piles of sweets of a larger kind, and by toys and dolls of all descriptions, suited to the youthful fancy. . . . On the summit of the tree stands the small figure of an angel, with outstretched wings, holding in each hand a wreath.

CHRISTMAS TREES

Violet Alleyn Storey

I saw along each noisy city street
The trees for Christmas, standing dark and still,
The pines and firs come down from field and hill,
Old trees and young that had known sun and sleet.

Soft needles fell on hard, dull pavement there,
And forest rose in a most treeless place;
And there was gladness in each passing face,
And there was balsam fragrance everywhere.

Oh, lovely way to celebrate Your Birth
Whose Birth Star glistened through Judea's trees;
Whom Joseph taught the skillful use of these;
Who, on a Tree, once overcame the earth!

Grant then Your blessing, Friend of Trees, we pray,
On those who deck green boughs for Christmas Day!

O Fir-tree green!
O Fir-tree green!
I still shall love you dearly!

—German Carol

THE LIGHT OF THE WORLD

Deck
the halls
with
boughs of
holly,
'Tis the
season
to be
jolly,

Each year at Christmastime, candles blaze in churches and homes across the world in honor of the birth of Jesus Christ, whose birth we celebrate at this time of year. The custom of placing candles in our windows follows a centuries-old tradition. The candles represent the hope that the Christ Child might be guided through the darkness to our homes. In ancient times, a stranger who approached a house lit by Christmas candles was assured of a warm welcome, for the families believed every visitor could be Christ Himself seeking refuge.

The Advent wreath also features candles, five in all: one for each week before Christmas and one for Christmas Day. The true old-fashioned Christmas or Yule Candle is rarely seen now. This candle of great proportions was able to burn for all of Christmas Day; if a candle's light was extinguished before the day ended, it was believed that bad luck was in store for the family in the months to come.

The Yule log, although not a candle, is a flame unique to Christmas and was central to the celebration in many European countries in days gone by. The new log was always brought in on Christmas Eve and kindled with the remainders of the previous year's log, which had been carefully preserved for twelve months. Oftentimes, the Yule logs were decorated with festive ribbons and evergreen boughs. Some French celebrants doused the log with wine; in other nations, Christians added wheat or unleavened bread to their Yule fire. The log was meant to burn for all the twelve days of Christmas.

Many of the old customs have passed out of favor, but the spirit behind them remains a part of modern Christmas celebration. Even today, the Christmas season is typified by lighted candles adorning table, mantel, and windowsill with a blazing fire in the hearth—and every flame is a reminder of the coming of Christ, the Light of the World.

Don
we now
our gay
apparel,
Troll the
ancient
Yuletide
carol,

See
the blazing
yule
before us,
Strike the
harp
and join the
chorus,

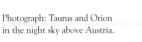

Photograph: Taurus and Orion
in the night sky above Austria.

THE STAR

Yorke Henderson

The star adorns the top of the Christmas tree, hangs from the lampposts, and graces the crèche upon our mantel. No other decoration of Christmas is so representative of the birth of Christ.

For centuries, Matthew's mention of a star mystified scholars. Although there is an abundance of astronomical records for the time, nowhere in them is there any mention of a new star. In 44 B.C. and in 17 B.C., brilliant comets were reported by watchers in the Mediterranean area. The next to be reported was not to be until A.D. 66. But around the supposed year of Jesus' birth there was no record of any significant astronomical phenomenon. Yet Matthew records the arrival in Bethlehem of "men who studied the stars" and their report of having seen a star. Was he merely repeating a legend that gave to the birth of his beloved Lord some of the glory he felt it should have had? That is not really likely. In an age when men were far more astronomically concerned than is the layman today, to invent a new star that no one else had seen would have been to invite discredit as a fanciful liar; and the lot of a Christian was hard enough in those days without courting unnecessary trouble.

Then what was the star whose existence Matthew reported? It was the great European mathematician and astronomer Johannes Kepler who first put his finger on a possible, and plausible, explanation. One night in 1603 Kepler was watching the approach of two planets, Saturn and Jupiter. Sometimes two planets move so close to each other that they give the viewer the impression of being a single large and brilliant star. It is what astrologers call a conjunction; and on that night Saturn and Jupiter were in conjunction. The sight triggered something in Kepler's mind, and he went back to his books. He was looking for a note written by the rabbinic scholar Abarbanel. According to Abarbanel, Jewish astrologers believed that the Messiah would appear when there was a conjunction of Saturn and Jupiter in the constellation Pisces. According to Kepler's astrological tables, there had been just such a conjunction in the year 6 B.C.

Follow
me in
merry
measure,
While I
tell of
Christmas
treasure.

—Welsh Carol

A Season of Light

The custom of placing candles in the windows of homes at Christmastime is a wonderful expression of the spirit of warmth and welcome that envelops Christians as they celebrate the birth of Christ. The candles announce to all who see the glimmer of their light that the weary traveller, the man, woman, or child in need of comfort and care, will find welcome within.

In 492 Candlemas Day was set aside as a day for blessing candles. This marked the end of Christmas celebrations, and greenery and decorations were removed from churches and homes. People brought candles to the church for blessing on this day and then kept them carefully through the year that followed, lighting them during times of illness or trial.

Star Boys are part of Christmas tradition in Sweden. On January 6, Star Boys, dressed as the three Wise Men, carry a paper star through the streets and sing Christmas carols.

Nowhere has the Christmas tree been longer a central part of Christmas than in Germany. So popular were Christmas trees, in fact, that in 1561, in Alsace, Germany, the government issued an order limiting the size of Christmas trees. Apparently, the forests were being depleted of their grander evergreens every December in the rush to cut and decorate the largest and most spectacular tree.

In an old Spanish tradition, children carried lamps through the streets on Christmas Eve to light the route for the journey of the Magi. In Germany, families left their houses dark to further highlight the brilliance of the candlelit Christmas tree.

In Ireland, families traditionally lighted their candles and left their doors wide open, a symbolic gesture to the Holy Family and a true invitation for all friends, family, and strangers to enter.

Candles were once lighted in the windows of the Catholic homes in Ireland so that the priest might sneak into the house during Christmas-tide and give Mass unbeknownst to the Protestant English. The Catholics would explain the signals by saying, "'Tis but our hope that Joseph and Mary will be looking for a spot to lie down and will see our candle and choose our home."

Each year, the citizens of Oslo, Norway, send a Christmas evergreen to stand in Trafalgar Square for the citizens of London. The custom originated during World War II when the King of Norway was exiled in England and missed the Christmases of his native land. Each year that the King remained in London, a Norwegian tree was smuggled through German lines to his home in England. Today, the tree is a symbol of the cooperation and good will between the two nations.

The Yule Log began during Medieval times when a stump or root was brought home on Christmas Eve and placed in the kitchen hearth or in the main fireplace. It was not to be bought, but obtained from one's own land. If it did not ignite immediately, trouble would follow for the year. In some areas the log was a whole tree cut up, bound, and drawn to the house by oxen. There it burned as people told tales of olden times, drank cider, and watched the dancing shadows on the wall.

In Poland, the Bethlehem star is at the center of Christmas celebrations. On Christmas Eve, a figure known as the Star Man delivers gifts to the children. Accompanied by his Star Boys, dressed as the Magi or the animals of the manger, Star Man first questions the children on their religious education and then presents each with a gift.

Light has been a part of Christmastime since even before there was a Christmas, back in the pre-Christian days when December celebrations were meant to drive away the fears of the dark mid-winter. Candles and fires burned to light the long, dark nights and symbolize the coming light of springtime. And when Christianity began to spread, the candles found a new significance as symbols of Jesus Christ, the new light of the world.

Various explanations have been put forth to explain, in scientific terms, the star of Bethlehem. It could possibly have been a comet, which blazed its path through the sky, leading the Magi to Bethlehem; but astronomers of the day, who knew of comets, made no mention in their records of such an event. The star might also have been a nova, which is an exploding star which becomes suddenly and spectacularly brilliant, but this theory has no scientific backing either. Most likely, the star was a conjunction of planets, like that observed by Johannes Kepler in the seventeenth century.

Jesus our brother, strong and good, Was humbly born in a stable rude, And the friendly beasts around Him stood, Jesus our brother, strong and good.

THE OXEN

Thomas Hardy

Christmas Eve, and twelve of the clock.
"Now they are all on their knees,"
An elder said as we sat in a flock
By the embers in hearthside ease.

We pictured the meek, mild creatures where
They dwelt in their strawy pen.
Nor did it occur to one of us there
To doubt they were kneeling then.

So fair a fancy few would weave
In these years! Yet, I feel,
If someone said on Christmas Eve,
"Come, see the oxen kneel

"In the lonely barton by yonder coomb
Our childhood used to know,"
I should go with him in the gloom
Hoping it might be so.

ATTENDANTS

David Morton

The mild-eyed Oxen and the gentle Ass,
    By manger or in pastures that they graze,
Lift their slow heads to watch us where we pass,
    A reminiscent wonder in their gaze.
Their low humility is like a crown,
    A grave distinction they have come to wear,—
Their look gone past us—to a little Town,
And a white miracle that happened there.

An old, old vision haunts those quiet eyes,
    Where proud remembrance drifts to them again,
Of Something that has made them humbly wise,
    These burden-bearers for the race of men—
And lightens every load they lift or pull,
Something that chanced because the Inn was full.

Opposite: *Winter*, Myles Birket Foster, 1825–1899.

"I,"
said the
donkey, shaggy
and brown,
"I carried
His mother
up hill and
down,
I carried her
safely to
Bethlehem
town,
I," said
the donkey,
shaggy and
brown.

"I,"
said the cow,
all white
and red,
"I gave
Him my
manger
for a bed; I
gave Him
my hay
to pillow His
head.
I," said the
cow, all
white and
red.

Shepherds, St. John's
Cathedral, Winnipeg,
Manitoba.

THE TRADITION OF THE MANGER SCENE

The beloved manger scene which adorns Christian homes each Christmas season traces its beginnings back to Francis of Assisi, who wanted to humanize the teachings of the scriptures and to remind Christians of the humble beginnings of Jesus Christ, their Saviour.

In 1224, Francis conceived his plan for a living manger scene while watching shepherds in a field outside the village of Greccio, Italy. He went to the Pope himself to seek permission to perform his Nativity scene and then sought help from a wealthy nobleman named Giovanni of Greccio, who Francis knew, "valued nobility of blood less than nobility of soul." Giovanni gave Francis the space in a hillside cave outside the village for his manger scene.

Before Christmas came, news spread through the countryside that Francis was planning a unique and special Christmas observance. After darkness on Christmas Eve, the villagers lit torches and walked up through the trees toward the manger, bringing the hillside alive with their bright light. Francis read the words of the Gospel which described the birth of Jesus in Bethlehem, and the crowd was awestruck, moved to silence by the beauty and simplicity of the moment. Legend tells that those present saw the vision of Francis cradling the Christ Child in his arms, surrounded by a supernatural light. The gathered Christians left the manger singing hymns and carried their torches back into the village. The beauty of the night was not soon forgotten by those who had witnessed it. Many understood the true meaning of the birth in the stable in Bethlehem fully for the first time that night. Thereafter, a living manger scene or a set of carved figures became increasingly part of the Christmas tradition in Italy, and eventually spread to many other Christian lands.

"I," said the sheep with curly horn, "I gave Him my wool for His blanket warm, He wore my coat on Christmas morn. I" said the sheep with curly horn.

"I,"
said the dove, from the rafters high, "Cooed Him to sleep that He should not cry; We cooed Him to sleep, my mate and I. I," said the dove from the rafters high.

NEIGHBORS OF THE CHRIST NIGHT

Nora Archibald Smith

Deep in the shelter of the cave,
  The ass with drooping head
Stood weary in the shadow, where
  His master's hand had led.
About the manger oxen lay,
  Bending a wide-eyed gaze
Upon the little new-born Babe,
  Half worship, half amaze.
High in the roof the doves were set,
  And cooed there, soft and mild,
Yet not so sweet as, in the hay,
  The Mother to her Child.

The gentle cows breathed fragrant breath
  To keep Babe Jesus warm,
While loud and clear, o'er hill and dale,
  The cocks crowed, "Christ is born!"
Out in the fields, beneath the stars,
  The young lambs sleeping lay,
And dreamed that in the manger slept
  Another white as they.

These were Thy neighbors, Christmas Child;
  To Thee their love was given,
For in Thy baby face there shone
  The wonder-light of Heaven.

Country Scene, nineteenth century, Artist Unknown.

A Lamb Conceals the Christ Child

John N. Then

The message that Christ was born spread fast and wide throughout the land. Herod, the king, was much alarmed and exceedingly jealous because he was told that the newborn Babe was hailed as the "King" of kings. He ordered all infants under two years old to be massacred, thinking in this way that the newborn Christ would be among them. Terrible it was to hear the heart-rending cries of the mothers as their babes were torn from their bosoms and brutally slaughtered. Although the murderers slew thousands of innocent children, they were not positive that the sought-for Christ Child was one of them.

To satisfy himself, therefore, Herod ordered some hirelings to return and thoroughly search the stable where the Babe was born. Stealthily they approached and looking through a crack in the wooden door, beheld a Child in the manger within. They forced the door open and rushed in, but the Child was gone. A frightened lamb ran across the straw. "What is this?" said they. "Did we not see the Child with our own eyes?" and they turned the straw over a hundred times and looked under the roof and in every nook and corner. The Child had disappeared. "What became of it?"

As the murderous soldiers of Herod neared the stable, there was great confusion and noise. Joseph and Mary were hurriedly making what arrangements they possibly could to flee to Egypt. The Babe in the manger, too, was disturbed and slipped out. A little lamb near by seemed to understand it all and quietly came over to the Christ Child bleating, "I will hide You" and gently covered Him like a canopy while the heavenly Babe clung fast to the long white fleece beneath.

Just then the soldiers burst open the door of the stable and began their search for the Babe, which they had seen as they peeked through the crack a few moments before. But in vain was their search, for no sooner had they entered, than the lamb with his precious burden passed them unnoticed and went out. And so the Christ Child was saved from the wrath of Herod.

Thus
every beast
by some good
spell,
In the
stable dark
was glad
to tell,
Of the
gift
he gave
Emmanuel,
The gift
he gave
Emmanuel.

—12th century

THE MANGER SCENE

Nativity scenes are one of the most cherished of Christmas traditions and can be seen in homes and in churches the world over. After Francis of Assisi introduced the idea in Italy, the nativity scene was adopted by Christians everywhere; but it remained most central to the Christmas celebration in southern Europe, where the symbolism of greens and evergreen trees—so important in the cold northern nations—held less meaning due to mild winter. The city of Naples became especially known for its beautiful hand-carved nativity scenes, a tradition begun in the eighteenth century by a nobleman of Naples.

Many animals are said to have been forever altered by witnessing the birth of Christ and the actions at the manger. The cattle, who kneeled in adoration in front of the Infant's crib, are to this day the only domestic beast to kneel before lying down. The nightingale is said to have learned its sweet song by singing to the baby Jesus when His mother's song was not able to soothe Him. And the robin's breast has been red, legend tells, ever since a tiny robin devotedly fanned the flames of the dying fire that was warming the tiny Baby in the manger.

In Italy, the nativity scene is called the PRESEPIO; in France, it is the CRÈCHE; in Germany the KRIPPE, and in Spain and much of Latin America, the NACIMIENTO.

Many legends tell of the rooster, who, it is said, has only one time in all the ages crowed at midnight, and that was the night of the birth of Jesus. In Spain, the rooster is honored each Christmas Eve with the MISA DEL GALLO, or the midnight Mass of the Rooster.

A charming ancient legend in many countries tells that on each Christmas Eve, animals are given the gift of speech, just as they were on the night of the nativity. Humans beings are warned not to try and listen to this sacred speech, as misfortune will surely befall all who do.

The legend of the straw and hay tells that when Mary wrapped her Babe in swaddling clothes and laid Him in the manger on a bed of straw and hay, the holy presence of the Child caused the hay and straw to come to life and produce a wreath of beautiful blossoms for Jesus' head. Mixed in with the straw and hay was also some dried fern, which, unmoved by the presence of the Christ Child, did not blossom. Because of this, the fern was condemned to a life without colorful blossoms and a habitat only in the darkest, coolest spots in the forest.

In medieval plays and carols, the animals of Bethlehem were each said to respond a certain way when told of the Christ Child's arrival. The rooster crowed out "CHRISTUS NATUS EST," which is Latin for "Christ is born." The ox mused "UBI," meaning "Where?" The sheep bleated "Bethlehem!" The donkeys brayed "EAMUS," or "Let's go!" The young calf replied, "VOLO," or "I'm going!"

In Italy during the nine days preceding Christmas (the novena), bagpipers go from house to house and play before the mangers. Some are dressed as shepherds and sing the shepherd song, CANTATA DEI PASTORI. They are rewarded with gifts of food or money.

At Christmastime, in several central-European countries, singing children walk through the streets in groups carrying a box containing a small nativity scene.

From the earliest times, paintings, songs, and poems about the nativity have told of the donkey Mary rode into Bethlehem and the ox and ass at the stable. However, the Gospels never mention what animal, if any, Mary rode, or any beasts that may have been present at the stable. The tradition of using the ox and ass, and perhaps the donkey as well, stems from Isaiah 1:3, "The ox knoweth his owner, and the ass his master's crib."

In Germany an especially endearing custom was that of cradle rocking. A manger scene was set up in churches; and during Christmas services, altar boys would gently rock the crib and sing soft carols and lullabies to the Infant within. The tradition died out when the Reformation banned such symbols inside the church, but it has remained in some small villages to this day.

CHRISTMAS FEAST

I n no other facet of Christmas is there such a rich and sumptuous heritage as in the traditions of holiday fare. This yearly celebration has demanded a table extended with family and friends and groaning under the load of rich candies, fruit-filled puddings, glazed sweet breads, roasted meats and fowl, every kind of vegetable, and, of course, decorated, squeezed, rolled, filled, cut, and iced cookies from almost every country in the world. As children, we each become so entranced with the smells of roasting turkey, baking pumpkin pies, or steaming plum puddings that thereafter, for the rest of our lives, only a slight whiff of a certain odor instantly unlocks the treasures of our memory as we are transported back to those wonderful Christmas feasts at home with Mother, Father, and our family of childhood.

A Sketch for "Many Happy Returns of the Day,"
William Powell Frith, 1819–1909.

Now Christmas is come,
Let's beat up the drum,
And call all our
neighbors together.
And when they appear,
Let us make them such cheer,
As will keep out the wind
and the weather.
—Washington Irving

THE CHRISTMAS TABLE

So, now
is come
our joyful
feast,
Let every
soul be
jolly!
Each room
with ivy
leaves is
drest,
And every
post with
holly.

Since its very beginnings, the Christmas holiday has brought people together to share in the celebration of Jesus' birth; and when people gather together to celebrate, there is always a feast. The English had the goose or roast beef at the center of their Christmas table, and the Germans featured suckling pigs. In America, the turkey has always been the favorite main course for Christmas. Native to American soil, the turkey has traditionally been stuffed with oyster dressing in homes on the East coast, whereas in the South the dressing of choice has been Southern cornbread. In many parts of the world, the Christmas meat or fowl is elaborately prepared in pies. The most famous pie in the annals of Christmas was that served at Sir Henry Grey's in London in 1770. The pie was nine feet in circumference and weighed twelve stone. It contained four geese, four wild ducks, two woodcocks, two turkeys, four partridges, seven blackbirds, six pigeons, two rabbits, two neats' tongues, two bushels of flour, twenty pounds of butter, and other items. Such a concoction gave credence to the English saying: "The Devil himself dare not appear in Cornwall during Christmas for fear of being baked in a pie."

Traditionally, mincemeat pies were filled with a savory mixture of meat, fowl, and spices which was meant to symbolize the gifts the Wise Men brought to the manger. The pies were formed into the oblong shape of a manger with an image of the baby Jesus on top. Because of this image, the pies were declared illegal by the ruling Puritans in England who saw the pies as idolatrous. In New England, Puritan settlers, unwilling perhaps to give up the wonderful taste of mincemeat, began to shape the pie in a traditional round shape and without the image of Jesus. After the Restoration in England when the monarchy supplanted the Puritan reign, some protestants still refused to eat mincemeat pie on a point of honor, illustrated by English minister John Bunyan's scorn when he was offered one in prison. Today, the mincemeat pie is not made of meat at all, but of raisins and other dried fruits.

Many of the delicious sweets we enjoy during the holidays originated in Germany. Filled with dried fruits and nuts, *Stollen,* or Christmas bread, has been a specialty of Dresden, Germany at Christmastime since the Middle Ages. *Springerle* is a cookie rolled out with a traditional springerle rolling pin engraved with a variety of Christmas symbols and pictures. *Lebkuchen,* German honey cakes, means literally "lively" cakes. These are often baked in elaborate, beautifully carved molds with paper pictures pasted on the top of the cakes. *Pfeffernüsse* is a traditional spice cookie with finely chopped candied fruit.

Almost every country in Christendom has a Christmas bread or cake, perhaps because bread is the staple of life; and many Christmas breads have interesting traditions behind them. Danish Kringle is an Advent bread shaped in the form of a pretzel. The "figgy pudding" we sing of at Christmas is actually a rich, dark fruitcake. *Roscon de Reyes*, or Three King Bread, from Spain is a sweet yeast bread filled with candied fruits and almonds; and *Panettone* is an Italian Christmas bread filled with raisins and lemon flavor. Saint Lucia's Crown is a double-tiered, braided coffee cake from Sweden which resembles a crown. Each year on St. Lucia's Day, December 13, the coffee cake is served at dawn with hot coffee to signal the opening of the Christmas season. But no bread or cake is as spectacular as the French *Bûche de Noël*, or Christmas Log, which is baked to resemble and recall to mind the Yule log of ancient days.

The Christmas feast is a sampling of the many cultures of the earth. It is also a symbol of the oneness of Christians the world over. For no matter what language they speak or what traditional rituals and celebrations they observe, all Christians are united at the Christmas table by the miracle at Bethlehem—the reason they have gathered and the reason they are feasting.

Though some churls at our mirth repine, Round your brows let garlands twine, Drown sorrow in a cup of wine, And let us all be merry!

Preparing Christmas Cookies and Cakes, Artist Unknown.

Now
all our
neighbours'
chimneys
smoke,
And
Christmas
logs are
burning;
Their
ovens
with baked
meats do
choke,
And all their
spits are
turning.

THE SKETCH BOOK

Washington Irving

The dinner was served up in the great hall, where the Squire always held his Christmas banquet. A blazing, crackling fire of logs had been heaped on to warm the spacious apartment, and the flame went sparkling and wreathing up the wide-mouthed chimney. . . .

We were ushered into this banqueting scene with the sound of minstrelsy; the old harper being seated on a stool beside the fireplace, and twanging his instrument with a vast deal more power than melody. Never did Christmas board display a more goodly and gracious assemblage of countenances; those who were not handsome were, at least, happy; and happiness is a rare improver of your hard-favoured visage. . . . The parson said grace, which was not a short familiar one, such as is commonly addressed to the deity, in these unceremonious days; but a long, courtly, well-worded one, of the ancient school. There was now a pause, as if something was expected, when suddenly the Butler entered the hall, with some degree of bustle; he was attended by a servant on each side with a large wax light, and bore a silver dish, on which was an enormous pig's head, decorated with rosemary, with a lemon in its mouth, which was placed with great formality at the head of the table. The moment this pageant made its appearance, the harper struck up a flourish; at the conclusion of which the young Oxonian, on receiving a hint from the squire, gave, with an air of the most comic gravity, an old carol. . . .

When the cloth was removed, the butler brought in a huge silver vessel of rare and curious workmanship, which he placed before the Squire. Its appearance was hailed with acclamation; being the Wassail Bowls so renowned in Christmas festivity. The contents had been prepared by the Squire himself; for it was a beverage in the skillful mixture of which he particularly prided himself; alleging that it was too abstruse and complex for the comprehension of an ordinary servant. It was a potation, indeed, that might well make the heart of a toper leap within him; being composed of the richest and raciest wines, highly spiced and sweetened, with roasted apples bobbing about the surface.

The old gentleman's whole countenance beamed with a serene look of indwelling delight, as he stirred this mighty bowl. Having raised it to his lips, with a hearty wish of a merry Christmas to all present, he sent it brimming round the board, for every one to follow his example, according to the primitive style; pronouncing it, "the ancient fountain of good feeling, where all hearts met together."

Without the door let sorrow lie, And if for cold it hap to die, We'll bury it in Christmas pie, And evermore be merry!

—George Wither

Opposite: *Princess Matilda's Dining Room, Courcelles Street in Paris*, Charles Giraud, 1819–1892.

The Christmas Feast

On Christmas morning in Colonial Virginia, breakfast was large and early followed by a fox hunt. Dinner was at half past three; food was abundant and included fish and foodstuffs from England, such as plum pudding and mince pie. Roast wild turkey came later.

Swedish tradition calls for a pause in Christmas feasting to remember a time of famine in the country's history. Families gather around a large kettle filled with broth into which they dip pieces of bread. This tradition, called "dipping in the kettle" is a means of giving thanks for the gifts of the season.

Long ago, in Provence, France, on Christmas Eve the most humble ate roast goose whereas the more well-to-do dined on turkey stuffed with sausage and black olives or truffles. Folk tradition says it was the goose's loud cackling that welcomed the Magi to the stable at Bethlehem. Peasants showed honor to the bird's hospitality when they ate goose at the supper to commemorate Jesus' birth.

In Holland, the children, in order to provide food and water for St. Nick's white horse on Christmas Eve, stuffed their clean wooden shoes with hay and carrots and placed them on the windowsill. A dish of water was often placed there too.

A typical Victorian Christmas feast in England began with a midday meal of soup, turkey, stuffing, plum pudding, and pie. At five o'clock, there would be a special tea; and at eight or nine o'clock, Christmas dinner would be served, complete with suckling pig, fish, cakes, and a variety of sweets.

In Poland, before the Christmas Eve meal is served, the master of the house distributes the peace wafers. These are small white wafers which are marked with scenes of the Nativity. Each member of the family shares his wafer with every other person at the table as a token of friendship and a symbol of peace on earth.

In Norway, a charming custom is the remembrance of the birds and animals, since they were in attendance at the birth of Christ. A specially gleaned sheaf of grain, saved from the fall harvest, is placed on top of a tall pole in the yard. On Christmas morning, every gable, gateway, and barn door is decorated with a bundle of grain for the birds' Christmas dinner.

In Sweden, Yuletide begins on December 13 with Saint Lucia's Day. Saint Lucia, represented by a young girl wearing a white dress, crimson sash, and a crown of leaves with white lighted candles, visits each household at dawn with a tray of coffee and cakes.

Engravings by
Randolph Caldecott,
from *The Sketch Book*.

In the Swedish countryside, people used to say the Lucia Bride, clothed in white and crowned with light, might be seen at dawn moving across the ice-bound lakes with food and drink for the parish poor.

Come,
guard this
night the
Christmas
Pie,
That the
Thiefe,
though
ne'er so
slie,
With his
Flesh-hooks
don't come
nie
To catch it

THE WASSAIL BOWL

The wassail bowl takes its name from the Anglo-Saxon term *waes hael*, which means "to be whole or hale." The custom of wassailing in England was originally an agricultural ritual focused on apple orchards. To honor the trees in the dead of winter, and to ensure a good crop for the following spring and summer, a wassail procession visited the orchards between Christmas and Epiphany. Singing and humming as they went, the wassailers carried a wassail bowl filled with a special mixture of mulled cider with apples and eggs which they sprinkled on the roots of selected trees. On occasion, the wassailers might even break the bowl against the trunk of a tree, much in the manner of christening a ship. With the passage of time, wassailing moved out of the orchards and into the village streets and became less about trees and more about celebrating the Christmas holiday as wassailers traveled from house to house singing and sharing drinks from their bowl. Today, the wassail bowl can still be found in many homes at Christmas time, awaiting friends and family to share in its Christmas cheer.

MULLED CIDER WASSAIL

1	gallon apple cider
8	three-inch cinnamon sticks
4	apples, studded with cloves
10	allspice berries

In a large saucepan, combine cider, cinnamon sticks, apples, and allspice berries. Simmer 30 to 40 minutes. Serve hot. Makes 32 servings.

Opposite: *Glad Tidings*, William M. Spittle, 1858–1917.

From
him, who all
alone sits
there,
Having his
eyes still
in his
care,
And a deale
of nightly
feare,
To watch it.

Wassaile
the
Trees,
that they

may beare

You many a
Plum,
and many a
Peare;

INTERVIEW WITH A SOUTHERN LADY, CHRISTMAS 1907

Christmas, an old-fashioned Christmas! You folks know mighty little about it, because up to the war time Christmas lived down South. It was the day of days. We had the taste and smells of it. Never was, never will be such good eating again. And the things were nearly as good to look at as to eat—though we had never heard of orchids and never put a yard of ribbon on our tables. What we did put there was the best we had of everything—linen, china, silver, glass. And the dinner itself took up so much room there was none left for decorations, pure and simple.

But at dessert we came out strong—served our fruit, our oranges, apples and occasionally malaga grapes—we called them Sicily grapes—in tall openwork china bowls, white with gilt bands. Nuts came on the table in Wedgwood boats, our sweet homemade wine in gold stemmed glasses, our figs and raisins in the finest glass dishes we could muster.

But the Christmasiest thing of all was the egg nog. It was full man's size—but nobody slighted it. It began Christmas, in fact—about 4 o'clock in the morning.

We had turkey, of course, but no cranberries. Why should we bother with them when jellied apples were so much better and prettier?

We had cake pans in those days, to be sure, but never enough for the Christmas baking. It was a liberal education just to taste one of Mama's oven pound cakes. They were baked between live coals, with only a greased paper between them and the iron, but they came out the richest brown, innocent of scores or streaks, even if they were six inches thick and sixteen across. Fine grained and light as a feather—and so good you felt like crying when you realized you couldn't eat any more.

Mama made batter puddings—but on sufferance. What she reveled in was cheesecake—though she was fairly well affected toward sweet potato custard. She would have been perfectly happy in cooking if only she had been able somehow, someway, to grease butter and sweeten sugar.

Along with them went fried pies—made of sun-dried peaches, slowly stewed until very soft, mashed, sweetened liberally, then spread over rounds of crust and the unspread half turned over and pinched and the pie popped into boiling hot fat. In two minutes it was turned to brown the other side. A hundred was a good Christmas frying—and gone long before New Year. Our doctor boasted proudly that, "in good fettle, he could eat an acre of fried pies."

For
more or lesse
fruits
they will bring
As you doe
give
them
Wassailing.

—Robert Herrick

Photograph: Finley, Oregon.

ON THE FARM

Paul Engle

Now that the time has come wherein Our Saviour Christ was born, The larder's full of beef and pork, The granary's full of corn.

There are no dinners like that anymore: every item from the farm itself, with no deep-freezer, no car for driving into town for packaged food. The pies had been baked the day before, pumpkin, apple, and mince; as we ate them, we could look out the window and see the cornfield where the pumpkins grew, the trees from which the apples were picked. There was cottage cheese, with the dripping bag of curds still hanging from the cold cellar ceiling. The bread had been baked that morning, heating up the oven for the meat, and as my aunt hurried by I could smell in her apron the freshest of all odors with which the human nose is honored—bread straight from the oven. There would be a huge brown crock of beans with smoked pork from the hog butchered every November. We would see, beyond the crock, the broad black iron kettle in a corner of the barnyard, turned upside down, the innocent hogs stopping to scratch on it.

There would be every form of preserve: wild grape from the vines in the grove, crabapple jelly, wild blackberry and tame raspberry, strawberry from the bed in the garden, sweet and sour pickles with dill from the edge of the lane where it grew wild, pickles from the rind of the same watermelon we had cooled in the tank at the milkhouse and eaten on a hot September afternoon.

Cut into the slope of the hill behind the house, with a little door of its own, was the vegetable cellar, from which came carrots, turnips, cabbages, potatoes, squash. Sometimes my scared cousins were sent there for punishment, to sit in darkness and meditate on their sins; but never on Christmas Day. For days after such an ordeal, they could not endure biting into a carrot.

And of course there was the traditional sauerkraut, with flecks of caraway seed. I remember one Christmas Day, when a ten gallon crock of it in the basement, with a stone weighting down the lid, had blown up, driving the stone against the floor of the parlor, and my uncle had exclaimed, "Good God, the piano's fallen through the floor."

All the meat was from the home place, too. Turkey, of course, and most useful of all, the goose—the very one which had chased me the summer before, hissing and darting out its bill at the end of its curving neck like a feathered snake. Here was the universal bird of an older Christmas: its down was plucked, washed, and hung in bags in the barn to be put into pillows; its awkward body was roasted until the skin was crisp as a fine paper; and the grease from its carcass was melted down, a little camphor added, and rubbed on the coughing chests of young children. We ate, slept on, and wore that goose. . . .

And of course the trimmings were from the farm too: the hickory nut cake made with nuts gathered in the grove after the first frost and hulled by my cousins with yellowed hands; the black walnut cookies, sweeter than any taste; the fudge with butternuts crowding it. In the mornings we would be given a hammer, a flatiron, and a bowl of nuts to crack and pick out for the homemade ice cream. . . .

All families had their special Christmas food. Ours was called Dutch Bread, made from a dough halfway between bread and cake, stuffed with citron and every sort of nut from the farm—hazel, black walnut, hickory, butternut. A little round one was always baked for me in a Clabber Girl baking soda can, and my last act on Christmas Eve was to put it by the tree so that Santa Claus would find it and have a snack—after all, he'd come a long, cold way to our house. And every Christmas morning he would have eaten it. My aunt made the same Dutch Bread and we smeared over it the same butter she had been churning from their own Jersey (highest butter fat content) cream that same morning.

To eat in the same room where food is cooked—that is the way to thank the Lord for His abundance. The long table, with its different levels where additions had been made for the small fry, ran the length of the kitchen. The air was heavy with odors not only of food on plates but of the act of cooking itself, along with the metallic smell of heated iron from the hardworking Smoke Eater, and the whole stove offered us its yet uneaten prospects of more goose and untouched pies. To see the giblet gravy made and poured into a gravy boat, which had painted on its sides winter scenes of boys sliding and deer bounding over snow, is the surest way to overeat its swimming richness.

The warning for Christmas dinner was always an order to go to the milkhouse for cream, where we skimmed from the cooling pans of fresh milk the cream which had the same golden color as the flanks of the jersey cows which had given it. The last deed before eating was grinding the coffee beans in the little mill, adding that exotic odor to the more native ones of goose and spiced pumpkin pie. Then all would sit at the table, and my uncle would ask the grace, sometimes in German, but later, for the benefit of us ignorant children, in English: "Come, Lord Jesus, be our guest,/Share this food that you have blessed."

As
God
hath plenty
to thee sent,
Take
comfort
of thy labors,
And let it
never thee
repent,
To feast
thy needy
neighbors.

—Author
Unknown

GINGERBREAD COOKIES

Native to China and India, ginger has been used in cookery for centuries. Fourteenth-century Germans formed guilds of gingerbread artisans and used intricately carved molds to create gingerbread masterpieces for the aristocracy. It was the bakers of the 1600s who added molasses to their recipes and began the tradition of making gingerbread to celebrate the holidays. Years later in the eighteenth century, the Brothers Grimm told of a house "made of bread, with a roof of cake and windows of barley" in the story of Hansel and Gretel; and from then on, decorative gingerbread houses have been a special Christmas treat. This firm, dark gingerbread recipe is perfect for making either gingerbread men for the tree or gingerbread houses to decorate with the family.

½	cup butter, at room temperature
¾	cup granulated sugar
1	large egg
¼	cup dark molasses
3	tablespoons orange juice
3½	cups flour
1	teaspoon baking soda
1	teaspoon ground cinnamon
1	teaspoon ground ginger
½	teaspoon salt

In a large bowl, cream the butter with the sugar until fluffy. Add the egg, molasses, and orange juice; beat well and set aside. In a large bowl, sift together the flour, baking soda, cinnamon, ginger, and salt; add gradually to the butter mixture, blending well. Divide the dough in half and wrap each half in plastic wrap. Chill 1 hour or until the dough is firm enough to handle.

Preheat oven to 350° F. On a greased baking sheet, roll out one portion of the dough to ⅛ inch thick. (Keep the other portion refrigerated until ready to use.) Cut out desired patterns and remove the excess dough from the baking sheet with a metal spatula. Bake 10 minutes. Remove from oven; allow cookies to cool on baking sheet 1 minute. Remove cookies to racks lined with waxed paper to cool. Makes approximately 3 dozen cookies.

Run, run as fast you can! You can't catch me, I'm the gingerbread man!

—Children's Fairy Tale

Opposite: *Merry Christmas,* Artist Unknown.

Villagers

all, this
frosty tide,
Let your
doors swing
open
wide,
Though
wind may
follow, and
snow
beside,
Yet draw us
in by your
fire
to bide;

Opposite: *Home for Christmas*, 1784, Jean Louis Gerome Ferris.

CHRISTMAS STOLLEN

This traditional German Christmas bread is shaped like a folded oval. Full of fruits and nuts, it makes a delicious holiday gift.

4–4½	cups flour
2	one-ounce packages dry yeast
⅓	cup granulated sugar
1	teaspoon salt
½	cup milk
½	cup water
⅓	cup butter
2	eggs, lightly beaten
½	cup chopped, candied cherries
¼	cup chopped citron
¼	cup raisins
¼	cup chopped walnuts or pecans
1	tablespoon butter, softened
1	cup powdered sugar, sifted
1	teaspoon butter, softened
1–2	tablespoons maraschino cherry juice, warmed
	Additional cherries and nuts for garnish

In a large bowl, combine 2 cups flour, yeast, granulated sugar, and salt; mix well and set aside. In a medium saucepan, heat milk, water, and butter until warm (120° F to 130° F; butter does not need to melt). Add to flour mixture. Stir in eggs. With an electric mixer, blend at low speed until moistened; beat 3 minutes at medium speed. By hand, gradually stir in cherries, citron, raisins, walnuts, and enough remaining flour to make a firm dough. On a floured surface, knead until smooth and elastic, 5 to 8 minutes. Place in a greased bowl, turning to grease top. Cover; let rise in a warm place until light and doubled in size, about 1 hour.

Punch down dough. Divide into 2 parts. On a lightly floured surface, roll or pat each half into a 14-by-8-inch oval. Spread with 1 tablespoon softened butter. Fold in half lengthwise and curve into a crescent. Press folded edge firmly to partially seal. Place on greased baking sheet. Cover; let rise in warm place until doubled in size, about 30 minutes. Preheat oven to 350° F. Bake 25 to 30 minutes until golden brown. Remove from baking sheets; cool.

In a small bowl, combine powdered sugar, 1 teaspoon softened butter, and maraschino cherry juice. Blend until smooth. Drizzle glaze over loaves. Garnish with additional cherries and nuts. Makes 2 small stollens.

Joy
shall be
yours in the
morning!

—Kenneth
Grahame

This is the week when Christmas comes. Let every pudding burst with plums,

PLUM PUDDING

Illustrated London News, 1848

In a household where there are five or six children, the eldest not above ten or eleven, the making of the pudding is indeed an event. It is thought of days, if not weeks, before. To be allowed to share in the noble work is a prize for young ambition. . . . Lo! the lid is raised, curiosity stands on tiptoe, eyes sparkle with anticipation, little hands are clapped in ecstasy, almost too great to find expression in words. The hour arrives—the moment wished and feared; envious fate should not allow it to be an event, and mar the glorious concoction in its very birth.

And then when it is dished, when all fears of this kind are over, when the roast beef has been removed, when the pudding, in all the glory of its own splendour, shines upon the table, how eager is the anticipation of the near delight! How beautifully it steams! How delicious it smells! How round it is! A kiss is round, the horizon is round, the earth is round, the moon is round, the sun and stars, and all the host of heaven are round. So is plum pudding.

STEAMED PLUM PUDDING

Originating in seventeenth-century England, plum pudding was a porridge of meat, dried fruits, rum, brandy, sugar, spices, butter, and eggs (and no plums whatsoever!). The puddings cooked slowly, for hours or even days, in great copper kettles over the open fire. Their presentation at the end of the Christmas feast was the highlight of the day.

1½	cups seedless raisins		1	teaspoon ground cinnamon
½	cup dried currants		½	teaspoon allspice
½	cup mixed candied fruit, finely chopped		¼	teaspoon ground nutmeg
1	tart apple, peeled, cored, and grated fine		1	cup fine dry bread crumbs
	Rind of 1 lemon, finely grated		1	cup firmly packed dark brown sugar
	Rind of 1 orange, finely grated		⅓	cup molasses
¾	cup orange juice		1	cup finely ground suet or softened butter
1	cup sifted flour		3	eggs, lightly beaten
1	teaspoon baking powder		½	cup chopped almonds
½	teaspoon salt		¼	cup brandy (optional)

In a large bowl, mix fruits, rinds, and orange juice; let stand ½ hour. In a large bowl, sift flour with baking powder, salt, and spices. Stir in all remaining ingredients. Add fruit mixture and mix well. Spoon into 2 well-greased, 1-quart pudding molds and cover tightly with lids or a double thickness of aluminum foil tied firmly in place. Set molds on a rack in a large stock pot. Add enough boiling water to the stock pot to boil. Cover and steam 4 hours; keep water simmering slowly. Remove puddings to another rack to cool before serving. (Or refrigerate until needed and reheat by steaming as before for 1 hour or by unmolding and heating in microwave.) Unmold warm puddings on to a hot platter. Pour warm brandy over top of pudding and light. Serve with pudding sauce (below). Makes 12 servings.

PUDDING SAUCE

½	cup butter, softened		⅛	teaspoon salt
2	cups sifted confectioners' sugar		1	tablespoon hot water
			1	teaspoon vanilla

In a small bowl, beat butter until creamy. Gradually beat in sugar, a little at a time. Beat in remaining ingredients and continue to beat until fluffy. Serve chilled or at room temperature. Makes about 1 cup.

And every tree bear **dolls** and **drums,** In the week when Christmas comes.

—Eleanor Farjeon

Opposite: *Christmas Comes But Once a Year*, 1896, Artist Unknown,

A man
might then
behold
At
Christmas,
in each hall,
Good fires
to curb
the cold,
And meat for
great
and small.

—Thomas Hood

THE CHRISTMAS GOOSE

Charles Dickens

You might have thought a goose the rarest of all birds; a feathered phenomenon, to which a black swan was a matter of course; and in truth, it was something like it in that house. Mrs. Cratchit made the gravy (ready before-hand in a little saucepan) hissing hot; Master Peter mashed the potatoes with incredible vigor; Miss Belinda sweetened up the applesauce; Martha dusted the hot plates; Bob took Tiny Tim beside him in a tiny corner, at the table; the two young Cratchits set chairs for everybody, not forgetting themselves, and mounting guard upon their posts, crammed spoons into their mouths, lest they should shriek for goose before their turn came to be helped. At last the dishes were set on, and grace was said. It was succeeded by a breathless pause, as Mrs. Cratchit, looking slowly all along the carving knife, prepared to plunge it in the breast; but when she did, and when the long-expected gush of stuffing issued forth, one murmur of delight arose all around the board, and even Tiny Tim, excited by the two young Cratchits, beat on the table with the handle of his knife, and feebly cried hurrah!

There was never such a goose. Bob said he didn't believe there was ever such a goose cooked. Its tenderness and flavor, size and cheapness, were the themes of universal admiration. Eked out by the applesauce and mashed potatoes, it was a sufficient dinner for the whole family; indeed, as Mrs. Cratchit said with great delight (surveying one small atom of a bone on the dish), they hadn't ate it all at last! Yet every one had had enough, and the youngest Cratchits in particular were steeped in sage and onion to the eyebrows! But now, the plates being changed by Miss Belinda, Mrs. Cratchit left the room alone—too nervous to bear witnesses—to take the pudding up, and bring it in.

Suppose it should not be done enough! Suppose it should break in turning out! Suppose somebody should have got over the wall of the backyard, and stolen it, while they were merry with the goose; a supposition at which the two young Cratchits became livid! All sorts of horrors were supposed.

Hallo! A great deal of steam! The pudding was out of the copper. . . . In half a minute Mrs. Cratchit entered, flushed, but smiling proudly, with the pudding like a speckled cannon-ball, so hard and firm, blazing in half of a half-a-quartern of ignited brandy, and bedight with Christmas holly stuck into the top.

Oh, a wonderful pudding! Bob Cratchit said, and calmly, too, that he regarded it as the greatest success achieved by Mrs. Cratchit since their marriage. Mrs. Cratchit said that now the weight was off her mind, she would confess she had had her doubts about the quantity of flour. Everybody had something to say about it, but nobody said or thought it was at all a small pudding for so large a family. It would have been flat heresy to do so. Any Cratchit would have blushed to hint at such a thing.

At last the dinner was all done, the cloth was cleared, the hearth swept, and the fire made up. . . . Then all the Cratchit family drew round the hearth, . . . while the chestnuts on the fire sputtered and cracked noisily. Then Bob proposed:

"A merry Christmas to us all, my dears. God bless us all!"

Which all the family re-echoed.

"God bless us every one!" said Tiny Tim, the last of all.

May the
fire of
this log
warm
the cold;
may the
hungry be fed;
may the
weary find
rest,
and may all
enjoy
heaven's
peace.

—Traditional
Prayer

Dickens's Christmas Carol, Bob Cratchit and Tiny Tim, Artist Unknown.

CHRISTMAS MUSIC

The days and nights of the Christmas season are alive with music. In churches, on street corners, on doorsteps, and at the family fireside, voices join together and are lifted in praise and celebration of the season. The roots of the popular carol stem from common folk displaying the joy of the holidays and spirits full of happiness; whereas the great oratorios, seasonal ballets, and moving hymns that mark the season were written in a state of euphoria and celebration, each note an echo of the song sung by the angels to the shepherds in the fields on that night two thousand years ago.

Winter on the Skating Pond in Central Park,
Currier and Ives, 1857–1907.

Then let your hearts be filled with joy,
While Christmas bells are ringing,
And keep the birthday of the Lord
With merriment and singing.
—Mary Jane Carr

There's
a song
in the air!
There's a
star
in the sky!
There's a
mother's
deep
prayer
And a
baby's
low cry!

THE HISTORY OF THE CHRISTMAS CAROL

"On Christmas night all Christians sing, To hear the news the angels bring," says a timeless carol from Sussex. The authentic carol is truly a folk song and has its beginnings in the traditional ring dance. The rhythmic beat of these joyous dances is evident in carols such as "I Saw Three Ships Come Sailing In." The air of celebration is in honor of Christ's birth and echoes the results of the fruits of the Spirit, certainly joy, about which the Apostle Paul spoke in Galatians 5:22.

It was not until the fifteenth century, however, that true carols originated in England, and the songs were a refreshing change from the rigid Latin hymns sung in England's churches and cathedrals. The oldest collection of printed carols dates back to 1521 and an even larger collection to 1550. Today, these same carols, which include "In Bethlehem That Fair City," "The First Good Joy That Mary Had," and "The First Noel," sound as joyful to our ears as they did four hundred years ago.

During England's Puritan era of approximately a decade, which ended in 1660, the carol survived only by going underground since anything associated with the celebration of Christmas was strictly forbidden. A Puritan tract of 1656 says, "No one thing more hindereth the Gospel work all the year long than doth the observation of that Idol Day once in a year, having so many days of cursed observation with it." During this time, throughout England, carols were heard only rarely and were not printed. After the Puritan era ended, carols were once again written and sung with unrestrained joy and survived to become a festive part of our modern Christmas celebrations.

THE FIRST GOOD JOY
THAT MARY HAD

"The First Good Joy" weds a tune of unknown origin with fifteenth-century verses describing the joy of the mother of Christ as she recognizes the divinity of her Son throughout His lifetime. Although the words are truly religious, the music has had many secular incarnations through the years. Several sources cite use of this melody by the unemployed of London in the nineteenth century, and more than one music historian recalls the tune as one used in several children's play songs.

1. The first good joy that Ma - ry had,— It was the joy— of
2. The next good joy that Ma - ry had,— It was the joy— of

one,———— To see the bless - ed Je - sus Christ When
two,———— To see her own son Je - sus Christ To

he was first— her son.——— When he was first her
make the lame— to go.——— To make the lame to

son, good man; And bless - ed may he be,——— Both
go, good man; And bless - ed may he be,——— Both

Fa - ther, Son and Ho - ly Ghost, To all e - ter - ni - ty.———

And
the star
rains its
fire
while the
Beautiful
sing,
For the
manger
of Bethlehem
cradles a
king.

—Josiah Gilbert
Holland

Calm
on the
listening ear
of night
Come
heaven's
melodious
strains,
Where wild
Judea
stretches far
Her
silver-
mantled
plains;

I SAW THREE SHIPS

More than three hundred years old, this English song has musical roots in the ancient songs sung to accompany ring dances—the first carols. The image of three ships is thought to trace back to the three ships which carried the remains of the three wise men to the city of Cologne in the twelfth century. Through the ages, legend replaced the wise men on board the ships with the figures of Mary, Joseph, and the Christ Child.

1.I saw three ships—— come sail - ing in, On
2.And what was in—— those ships all three? On
3.Our Sa - viour Christ—— and his la - dy, On
4.O, they sailed in - to Beth - le - hem, On
5.And all the an - gels in heaven shall sing, On

Christ-mas Day, on Christ-mas Day; I saw three ships—— come
Christ-mas Day, on Christ-mas Day, And what was in—— those
Christ-mas Day, on Christ-mas Day, Our Sa - viour Christ—— and
Christ-mas Day, on Christ-mas Day, O, they sailed in - to
Christ-mas Day, on Christ-mas Day, And all the an - gels in

sail - ing in On Christ-mas Day in the morn - ing.
ships all three On Christ-mas Day in the morn - ing?
his la - dy, On Christ-mas Day in the morn - ing.
Beth - le - hem, On Christ-mas Day in the morn - ing.
heaven shall sing, On Christ-mas Day in the morn - ing.

Celestial choirs from courts above Shed **sacred** glories there; And angels with their sparkling lyres Make music on the air.

—Edmund Hamilton Sears

Who
can
forget—
forget—
never to be
forgot—
The **time,**
that all the
world in
slumber lies,

When, like the
stars,
the singing
angels shot
To earth,
and heaven
awakèd
all his eyes
To see another
sun
at midnight
rise.

—Giles Fletcher

*The Annunciation
to the Shepherds,*
1656, Nicolaes Pietersz
Berchem, 1620–1683.

The Messiah

Gerard and Patricia Del Re

Glory

to God

in the

highest,

and peace

on earth,

goodwill

towards

men.

On August 22, 1741, George Frederick Handel began to act strangely. He shut himself into his room, sat at his desk, and almost did not eat or sleep for three weeks while he worked. When his servants tried to get him to eat, he would flare up at them, eyes blazing. If he ate, he continued to work with the hand that didn't hold the bread. He behaved like a madman, and perhaps he was—divinely mad.

The German-born Handel came to London in 1710 at the age of twenty-five. He immediately became the toast of the town when his opera *Rinaldo* proved to be a big success. Always a prolific composer, he turned out dozens of the popular Italian operas that the aristocratic audience clamored for. But in 1728 disaster struck—in a most unlikely form. A rowdy work called *The Beggar's Opera* was produced in London. A risqué satire on Italian opera and current politics, it contained a score made up of a host of popular tunes of the day (including one from one of Handel's operas) fitted out with new words. It was a smash hit. This was something the common people could enjoy, without having to know Italian or the conventions of the stilted operatic format of the time. Italian opera and its prime composer, Handel, began struggling for its life.

One of the steps Handel took to try to regain popularity was the composition of oratorios. The oratorio was a different format from opera in that the work was not staged, so it did not have to be specifically dramatic and it could be composed in English, which no serious opera of the time could be. He produced fifteen of these in the years leading up to 1741 with varying success. The fickleness of the public was a source of great disappointment to him, and the once-lionized composer found himself being treated as an old-timer. Financially, he was in difficult straits.

When his fit of mad composition came upon him in 1741, he did not even have a commission that he was working on. The new work that he was composing might never be performed for all he knew at the time. It did not matter. It was a different, higher voice than that of the public which he was listening to as the days passed without food and rest.

A servant found him one day weeping at his desk. He rushed forward to help, but Handel looked up at him with a great light shining through the tears of his eyes. "I did think I did see all Heaven before me, and the great God Himself," he said. He had just completed the "Hallelujah Chorus."

Messiah was completed in twenty-four days, an incredibly short time for a work that takes nearly three hours to perform in its entirety. The completed manuscript was then put aside for the next seven weeks. Finally the Lord Lieutenant of Ireland asked him to visit Dublin and give some charity concerts there. He brought [the new work] with him. On April 13, 1742, the first performance of the *Messiah* was given in Dublin. . . .

Today the *Messiah* is thought of as a Christmas work; at least, that is when most performances of it are presented. Actually, the work is divided into three sections, only the first of which deals with Christmas. Starting with the prophecies about Christ's birth, the first part is highlighted by the joyous chorus "For unto Us a Child Is Born" and the angels' song to the shepherds. There is very little actual narrative, being more descriptions of the emotions produced by the joyous tidings. The second part tells of Christ's Crucifixion and Resurrection, again without actually telling a story. The second part ends with the "Hallelujah Chorus" and is often referred to as the Easter section, the first part being called the Christmas section. The third part is a contemplation on the meaning of Christ's ministry and its promise of resurrection for all believers. . . .

The *Messiah* is one of the supreme achievements of human art. Its polyphonic writing, the weaving of melody against melody in the different voice and instrument parts, has few equals in all the world of music; and the lyricism of its gentle airs is truly touching. But it goes beyond the bounds of mere ability and rises to inspiration. As Milton Cross puts it, "Never a religious man in the same sense as Bach, Handel became the God-intoxicated man while writing *Messiah*." Sheer joy and glory fill the whole work and make it especially appropriate to the Christmas season when the joy of Christ's birth fills all our hearts.

Original manuscript
of the *Messiah*,
by George
Frederick Handel.

Rejoice greatly, O daughter of Zion! Shout! O daughter of Jerusalem Behold, thy King cometh unto thee!

—from the MESSIAH,
George Frederick
Handel

MUSIC FROM THE REALMS OF GLORY

Afraid to trust the London critics with his new oratorio, Handel first conducted the MESSIAH himself, in Dublin, Ireland, on Tuesday morning, April 13, 1742. At its first London performance, King George II stood up during the "Hallelujah Chorus," a tradition that continues today throughout the world.

Our custom of caroling most likely came from Medieval England when a chorus of singers, called waits, held licenses to sing, day or night, to function sort of as the municipal voice at any and all functions, from the visits of dignitaries to weddings. They were especially busy during Christmastime, at feasts or caroling, telling the story of the nativity in song.

A 1918 survey conducted by the National Bureau for the Advancement of Music reported that community singing, or caroling, was alive in thirty American cities. By 1928, the same society reported that more than 2,000 cities had community singing.

An old legend states that upon the stroke of midnight on the night Jesus Christ was born, all of the bells in the world suddenly began ringing of their own accord, and no sound before or since could match the majesty of the sound.

Phillips Brooks, pastor of Holy Trinity Church in Philadelphia, wrote "O Little Town of Bethlehem" after being inspired by a trip to the Holy Land, when on Christmas Eve he had looked down on the lights of the city of Bethlehem.

The New York WORLD in 1898 reported a revival of caroling in Hackensack, New Jersey, when before sunrise on Christmas morning, men and women went about the town in a wagon drawn by four horses and sang carols in front of the homes of friends.

NOEL comes from the French word for Christmas, which in turn stems from the Latin NATALIS, meaning "birthday." "The First Noel," a French carol, probably dates from as early as the thirteenth or fourteenth century and was most likely sung in the miracle plays that told stories of the Bible dramatically and in the vernacular of the common people.

Joseph Mohr, rector of the village church at Obendorf, Austria, asked Franz Gruber to write a tune for a poem Mohr had just written. Gruber had to pick out the melody on an old guitar because the organ was broken. On December 25, 1818, the villagers of Obendorf gathered in the rectory to hear for the first time in a small church in a small village in the Tyrolean Alps of Austria, the song "Silent Night."

ENGRAVINGS BY RANDOLPH CALDECOTT, FROM THE SKETCH BOOK.

There really was a Good King Wenceslas (of the song by the same name), but he was not a king but rather a duke: the Duke of Bohemia. Although he was a good and honest man, as evidenced by the song about him, in A.D. 929 he was murdered by his envious and wicked younger brother.

Sound over all
waters,
reach out from
all lands,
The chorus of
voices, the
clasping of
hands;
Sing hymns that
were sung by
the stars
of the morn,
Sing songs
of the
angels
when Jesus
was born!

Opposite: *Merry Christmas,*
Maxfield Parrish, 1870–1966.

THE WASSAIL SONG

This happy carol is an Old English wassailing song that wishes good luck and good health to all. In fourteenth-century England, bands of beggars and orphans would dance through the cold and snowy streets of England offering to sing and to tell the householder's fortune if he would give them a drink from his wassail bowl, or a penny, or the privilege of standing a few minutes beside a warm fire.

1. Here we come a - was - sail-ing A - mong the leaves so
2. We are not dai - ly beg - gars That beg from door to
3. Good Mas - ter and good Mis - tress While you sit by the
4. God bless the mas - ter of this house, Like - wise the mis - tress

green, Here we come a - wand'ring, So fair to be seen:
door, But we are neigh-bors' chil-dren Whom you have seen be - fore:
fire, Pray think of us poor chil-dren A - wand-'ring in the mire:
too, And all the lit - tle chil-dren That 'round the ta - ble go:

CHORUS
Love and joy come to you, And to you your was - sail
too, And God bless you, and send you A hap - py new
year, And God send you A hap - py new year.

With glad
jubilations
Bring hope
to the
nations!

GOD REST YE MERRY, GENTLEMEN

This carol was first sung in the streets of London during the time of the traveling waits. In Charles Dickens's A Christmas Carol, Scrooge hears a caroler on the streets of London singing "God Rest Ye Merry, Gentlemen" and threatens to hit the singer with a ruler if he does not cease immediately. Of course, at the end of that night, Scrooge himself becomes a merry gentleman.

1. God rest ye mer-ry, gen-tle-men, Let noth-ing you dis-
2. In Beth-le-hem in Jew - ry This bless-ed Babe was
3. From God our heav-'nly Fa - ther A bless-ed an - gel
4. "Fear not, then," said the an - gel, "Let noth-ing you af-

may, Re - mem-ber Christ our Sav - iour Was born on Christ-mas
born, And laid with-in a man - ger, Up - on this bless-ed
came; And un - to cer - tain shep-herds Brought tid-ings of the
fright, This day is born a Sa - iour Of a pure Vir - gin

Day; To save us all from Sa-tan's pow'r When we were gone a-
morn; The which His moth-er Ma - ry Did noth-ing take in
same; How that in Beth-le - hem was born The son of God by
bright; To free all those who trust in Him From Sa-tan's pow'r and

stray.
scorn. O - ti - dings of com - fort and joy, com-fort and
name.
might.

joy; O - ti - dings of com - fort and joy.

Rise,
hope
of the ages,
arise like
the sun,
All speech
flow to
music,
all hearts
beat
as one!

Tchaikovsky's The Nutcracker

Sing the song of
great joy
that the
angels began,
Sing of glory to
God and
of good will
to man!

—John Greenleaf
Whittier

On December 17, 1892, a new ballet premiered on a stage in St. Petersburg, Russia. The crowd was less than impressed. For one thing, the story centered almost entirely on children, and for another, the music was not at all the traditional ballet music of the day. Audiences were accustomed to the music taking a backseat to the dancing in ballet; but in *The Nutcracker,* composer Peter Ilich Tchaikovsky had written beautiful and compelling symphonic music. In spite of the initially cool reception, *The Nutcracker* continued to be performed and went on to become one of the most popular ballets of all time, and certainly the world's favorite Christmas ballet.

The Nutcracker tells the story of a brother and a sister, Clara and Fritz, who receive some special and magical Christmas gifts, one of which is a delightful little nutcracker with a human form. Clara and Fritz cannot agree to share the nutcracker and go to bed with the issue unresolved. In darkness, Clara climbs from her bed to retrieve the nutcracker and comes upon a fantasy scene of toys and mice in battle. The toy soldiers, under the command of the prized nutcracker, are losing their battle with the King of the Mice and his own mice soldiers. Boldly, Clara throws her slipper at the mouse leader and wins the day for the toy soldiers. Her reward is a magical journey with the nutcracker—by then transformed into a handsome prince—to a land of fantasy called the Kingdom of Sweets, where she meets the Sugarplum Fairy. What follows is a scene of beautiful colors, energetic dancing, and special effects which, on stage, have proved endlessly captivating for audiences of all ages.

Tchaikovsky himself always expressed his dislike for this ballet, but his opinion has been overruled. Almost every major ballet company and countless small, amateur groups perform the ballet each December, and countless families have embraced the ballet as an essential part of their Christmas season.

Opposite: *Christmas Fancy Dress Party*, Percy Tarrant, nineteenth century.

Hear the
sledges
with the
bells,
Silver bells!
What a world
of merriment
their
melody
foretells!
How they
tinkle, tinkle,
tinkle,
In the icy air
of night!

WHY THE BELLS RING OUT

Christmas bells peal out the happy news of the Saviour's birth from the belfries of the grandest cathedrals, from the tiny steeples of humble country churches, and from the hands of carolers making their joyous rounds. Bells have been a part of Christian churches since the fifth century, when church bells began to be used in Italy to call worshippers to service. They were first heard in the churches of France in the middle of the sixth century; and in 680, the first church bell was rung in England by Benedict, Abbot of Weymouth. Soon missionaries carried bells to other parts of Britain; and a Saxon king, Egbert, is reported to have decreed that all church services be announced by ringing bells.

Because of their original association with churches, bells acquired a sacred character, and passages from the Bible were often engraved on them. One tenor bell, dedicated to St. Nicholas at a church in England, bore the inscription: "Pray for our children, pray for our sailors. Pray for this town. I to the church the living call and to the grave do summon all." The bells were treated with special respect and care by church members; and in some churches, the bells were actually given names, anointed, and baptized. In 1878, the chimes of London's St. Paul's Cathedral were blessed.

Bells were a familiar part of everyday life even in the days before the birth of Christ. Their ringing announced events of importance and enhanced special celebrations. And as Christianity spread, the ringing of church bells became a familiar sound to Christians the world over. Church bells still chime on many occasions throughout the year, but at no time is their sound so clear or their ring so joyous as when they sound out in celebration of the Christmas miracle.

Opposite: *Evening Service*,
Worthington Whittredge,
1820–1910.

While the
stars
that
oversprinkle
All the
heavens
seem to
twinkle
With a
crystalline
delight;

I HEARD THE BELLS
ON CHRISTMAS DAY

Keeping
time,
time, time,
In a sort
of Runic
rhyme,
To the
tintinnabulation
that so
musically
wells

This familiar song is an example of later carols, which were often poems set to music. In 1861, Henry Wadsworth Longfellow was facing the Christmas season with a heavy heart following the death of his wife and the outbreak of the American Civil War. As the Christmas bells pealed, their persistent and uplifting message inspired Longfellow to write a poem of his renewed faith. In the 1870s, his poem was set to music by English organist John Baptist Caulkin, and it is now one of our most beloved carols.

1. I heard the bells on Christ - mas day Their
2. I thought how, as the day had come, The
3. And in de - spair I bowed my head: "There
4. Then pealed the bells more loud and deep: "God
5. Till, ring - ing, sing - ing on its way, The

old fa - mi - iar car - ols play, And wild and sweet the
bel - fries of all Chris - ten - dom Had rolled a - long th'un -
is no peace on earth," I said, "For hate is strong, and
is not dead, nor doth He sleep; The wrong shall fail, the
world re - volved from night to day A voice, a chime, a

words re - peat Of peace on earth, good will to men.
bro - ken song Of peace on earth, good will to men.
mocks the song Of peace on earth, good will to men."
right pre - vail, With peace on earth, good will to men."
chant sub - lime, Of peace on earth, good will to men.

Opposite: *The Village Church in the Snow*, Charles Leaver, 1860–1884.

From the
bells, bells,
bells, bells,
Bells, bells,
bells—
From the
jingling
and the
tinkling
of the
bells.

—Edgar Allan Poe

The
earth
has grown
cold with its
burden of
care,
But at
Christmas
it always
is young.
The heart
of the jewel
burns lustrous
and fair,
And its
soul full of
music

THE SPIRITUAL

The Negro spiritual, although not limited to Christmas by any means, fits the mood of the holiday. To slaves in the United States, the birth of a Saviour who would set all men free was a miracle to be sung about. Unlike Euopean carols that trace their origins back to lively folk songs, the American Spiritual was born out of pain and misery.

Spirituals had been sung for generations and carried from plantation to plantation by oral tradition. It was not until the American Civil War that several of the traditional melodies were written down; and in 1867, a collection entitled *Slave Songs of the United States* was published.

RISE UP, SHEPHERD

This spiritual closely resembles a European shepherd carol. It brings to mind the voices of shepherds calling to one another from their lonely hilltops and alternates the lines of the lead singer with a group refrain as the news of the birth in a Bethlehem manger is spread across the countryside.

1.There's a   star   in   the   East   on
2.If   you   take   good   heed   to   the

Christ - mas   morn,   Rise   up,   shep- herd, and
an - gel's   words,   Rise   up,   shep- herd, and

fol - low.   It' - ll   lead   to the place   where the
fol - low.   You'll for - get   your   flocks,   you'll for -

breaks forth on
the air,
When the song
of the
Angels
is sung.
The feet
of the
humblest
may walk
in the
field
Where the feet
of the
holiest
have trod,

GO TELL IT ON THE MOUNTAIN

This authentic spiritual probably dates from the early 1800s. When there was something to tell, what better place to tell it from than a mountain, just as Jesus had chosen for His Sermon on the Mount. Indeed, "Go Tell It on the Mountain" takes its inspiration from Christ's sermon and urges the faithful to climb the highest mountaintop to proclaim the news of Jesus' birth.

Go tell it on the moun - tain,

o - ver the hills and ev - 'ry - where;— Go tell it on the

FINE

moun - tain that Je - sus Christ— is born.

1. When I was a seek - er, I sought both night and day; I
2. He made me a watch - man up - on the ci - ty wall; And

D.C.

sought the Lord to help me, And He showed me the way.
if I am a Christ - ian, I am the least of all.—

This, this
is the
marvel
to mortals
revealed,
When
the silvery
trumpets
of Christmas
have pealed,
That
mankind
are the
children of
God.

—Phillips Brooks

Opposite: *The Banjo Lesson,*
Henry O. Tanner, 1893.

GIFTS
AND
GREETINGS

T he giving of gifts was set by example, first by God in the gift of His Son, and then by the Magi who brought unusually precious gifts to the manger. Perhaps it was the cost of these first gifts of Christmas that inspires us today to give—to our family, to the poor, to strangers and friends alike—the best that we have to offer. Gift-giving has evolved to include assistants throughout the world, who bring gifts and candy to children after the youngsters are fast asleep. But whatever the tradition, whether through the Three Kings, the *Christkind*, or even St. Nicholas, the goal remains the same, and that is to bring joy and good will to those less fortunate or too young to do for themselves. And in the giving, we discover that offering our hearts to others brings the greatest joy of all.

Adoration of the Kings, Jean Tassel, 1608–1667.

For once, on a December night
An angel held a candle bright.
And led three wise men by its light
To where a Child was sleeping.
—Harriet F. Blodgett

GIVING GIFTS

What
can I give
Him,
Poor as I am?
If I were a
shepherd
I would
bring a
lamb,

As Isaiah prophesied, the first great gift was the gift of God's Son to mankind. After the nativity, the Magi responded in kind; and the gifts they laid at the Christ Child's crib remain a model for Christian gift giving at Christmastime to this day.

The pre-Christian Romans generally exchanged gifts as part of their winter solstice and new year celebrations. On New Year's Day, they would offer each other sweet pastry, precious stones, and even gold or silver as tokens of their good wishes. As Christianity took hold throughout the empire, these gift-giving customs were maintained but infused with new meaning: gifts were thereafter given in the name of the Christ child.

A traditional day for giving gifts in Britain, Boxing Day, originated from the feast of Saint Stephen, which was celebrated on December 26. On the day after Christmas in medieval times, the priests would empty the alms boxes in all the churches and distribute the gifts to the poor of the parish. Workers and servants kept their own personal "boxes," in which they saved throughout the year. At Christmas Day came the greatest and last flow of coins of the year. Then, on the day after Christmas, the box was broken and the money counted.

In many European countries, legends evolved of the Christ Child Himself as a Christmas gift giver. Unseen by the children, the Child would come, attended by a party of angels, to trim the tree and lay out gifts for the children. In Germany, the Christ Child was known as *Christkind*. Transplanted to America, *Christkind* became Kris Kringle, and Kris Kringle eventually became another name for the Dutch version of St. Nicholas, *Sinter Klaas*, or Santa Claus. Combining elements from the European Christ Child figures as well as from the many legends surrounding St. Nicholas, the American Santa Claus evolved into the jolly, red-suited elf who brings gifts to children at Christmastime.

The spirit of giving that has been a part of Christmas since its beginning manifests itself in many ways. Traditions of gift giving include acts of charity and good will toward family, friends, the community, and all who are in need. Out of our Christmas rejoicing at the birth of the Son of God is born a true spirit of humanity and generosity. The gift God gave to the world has begotten innumerable gifts, large and small, throughout the ages.

Opposite: *Christmas Greetings*,
Artist Unknown.

Christmas Greetings

If
I were a
Wise
Man,
I would
do my part;
Yet what I can
give Him,
Give my heart.

—Christina Rossetti

THE WISE MEN FROM THE EAST

Alfred Carl Hottes

We

three kings

of Orient are,

Bearing

gifts we

traverse

afar,

Field and

fountain,

moor and

mountain,

Following

yonder

star.

W ho were these Wise Men, these sages, and what wisdom did they have? From whence in the east did they come and where did they go? Do we know their names? To these questions the Bible gives us but scant answers. Legend, however, has clothed their lives with much to stir our fancies.

Before discussing the fascinating tales, let us again read the second chapter of the Gospel according to Matthew:

Now when Jesus was born in Bethlehem of Judea in the days of Herod the king, behold, there came wise men from the east to Jerusalem, saying, Where is he that is born King of the Jews? For we have seen his star in the east, and we are come to worship him. When Herod the king had heard these things, he was troubled, and all Jerusalem with him. And he sent them to Bethlehem and said, go and search diligently for the child. When they had heard the king they departed: and, lo, the star, which they saw in the east, went before them, till it came and stood over where the child was. And when they were come into the house, they saw the young child with Mary his mother, and fell down and worshiped him; and when they had opened their treasures, they presented unto him gifts; gold, and frankincense, and myrrh.

This is all we really know about the wise men. We believe they appeared to the Christ Child on January 6, on what is known as the Twelfth Night, or the Epiphany. They are called the Magi, which was a sect of priests among the ancient Medes and Persians, celebrated for their enchantments, their learning as astrologers, and for their great wisdom. It is from the Magi that we have the word "magic" given to the art of enchantment.

We do not know how many wise men there were, nor their names. St Augustine and St. Chrysostom say there were twelve, but common church tradition names three, no doubt because of the three gifts. Melchior, King of Arabia, sixty years old, brought a casket of gold in the form of a shrine, for he came from a country where the soil is ruddy. Gaspar, or Caspar, King of Tarsus, land of merchants, is often represented as a beardless youth of twenty; he is said to have brought myrrh in a gold-mounted horn. Balthazar, King of Ethiopia or Saba, land of spices, forty years old, reputedly of the black race, brought frankincense. Each of these gifts was considered symbolic or prophetic of what Jesus was to become—gold for a king, frankincense for a high priest, and myrrh for the great physician.

Born
a King on
Bethlehem's
plain,
Gold I bring
to crown
Him
again;
King forever,
ceasing never,
Over us all to
reign.

Photograph: Willamette
National Forest, Oregon.

Frankincense
to offer have I,
Incense
owns a
Deity nigh;
Prayer and
praising,
all men
raising,
Worship
Him,
God on high.

THE THREE KINGS

Henry Wadsworth Longfellow

Three Kings came riding from far away,
    Melchior and Gaspar and Balthazar;
Three Wise Men out of the East were they,
And they traveled by night and they slept by day,
    For their guide was a beautiful, wonderful star.

The star was so beautiful, large and clear,
    That all the other stars of the sky
Became a white mist in the atmosphere;
And by this they knew that the coming was near
    Of the Prince foretold in the prophecy.

Three caskets they bore on their saddle-bows,
    Three caskets of gold with golden keys;
Their robes were of crimson silk, with rows
Of bells and pomegranates and furbelows,
    Their turbans like blossoming almond-trees.

And so the Three Kings rode into the West,
    Through the dusk of night over hill and dell,
And sometimes they nodded with beard on breast,
And sometimes talked, as they paused to rest,
    With the people they met at some wayside well.

"Of the child that is born," said Balthazar,
    "Good people, I pray you, tell us the news;
For we in the East have seen his star,
And have ridden fast, and have ridden far,
    To find and worship the King of the Jews."

And the people answered, "You ask in vain;
    We know of no king but Herod the Great!"
They thought the Wise Men were men insane,
As they spurred their horses across the plain
    Like riders in haste who cannot wait.

And when they came to Jerusalem,
    Herod the Great, who had heard this thing,
Sent for the Wise Men and questioned them;
And said, "Go down unto Bethlehem,
    And bring me tidings of this new king."

So they rode away, and the star stood still,
 The only one in the gray of morn;
Yes, it stopped, it stood still of its own free will,
Right over Bethlehem on the hill,
 The city of David where Christ was born.

And the Three Kings rode through the gate and the guard,
 Through the silent street, till their horses turned
And neighed as they entered the great inn-yard;
But the windows were closed, and the doors were barred,
 And only a light in the stable burned.

And cradled there in the scented hay,
 In the air made sweet by the breath of kine,
The little Child in the manger lay,
The Child that would be King one day
 Of a kingdom not human, but divine.

His mother, Mary of Nazareth,
 Sat watching beside his place of rest,
Watching the even flow of his breath,
For the joy of life and the terror of death
 Were mingled together in her breast.

They laid their offerings at his feet:
 The gold was their tribute to a King;
The frankincense, with its odor sweet,
Was for the Priest, the Paraclete;
 The myrrh for the body's burying.

And the mother wondered and bowed her head,
 And sat as still as a statue of stone;
Her heart was troubled yet comforted,
Remembering what the angel had said
 Of an endless reign and of David's throne.

Then the Kings rode out of the city gate,
 With a clatter of hoofs in proud array;
But they went not back to Herod the Great,
For they knew his malice and feared his hate,
 And returned to their homes by another way.

Myrrh
is mine;
its bitter
perfume
Breathes a life
of gathering
gloom;
Sorrowing,
sighing,
bleeding, dying,
Sealed in the
stone-cold
tomb.

Glorious

now behold Him arise, King, and God, and Sacrifice; Alleluia, Alleluia, Earth to heav'n replies.

THE GIFT OF BETHLEHEM

John N. Then

For twenty-four months the Magi traveled together and the time of separation for Caspar had come. Watching Melchior and Balthazar proceed, he waited until he could see them no longer, then turned homeward. His thoughts were now of the home and family he had left two years ago and it was yet a two-day ride before he could reach them. He yearned for Ilzaide, his wife, and their son who would now be twelve years old, almost a man. Caspar rode steadily, and without mishap he entered the gates of his native city at sundown of the second day. The heavens were resplendent with brilliant colors of crimson-gold and purple of the sunset, and he took it for a happy omen. "Only a few paces more thou faithful Haboul," he cries to his horse, "and we are home." A moment later he was in the courtyard but no servants came to the gate. He pushed the gate open and entered. All seemed deserted. Then a sound of far-off wailing greeted his ears.

With fear in his heart, Caspar hurried down the corridor which led to the living rooms of his family. The wailing grew louder and he saw that it came from the servants huddled together at the entrance to one of the rooms. From them he learned that his son lay dying within the room. Caspar pushed aside the heavy silken hangings and stepped into the room. Lights were burning and the boy lay dying on a couch piled high with cushions, while the mother with clasped hands knelt by his side watching him. Caspar drew near but she did not raise her eyes.

"Thou art in time to see thy boy die," said she.

Falling on his knees, Caspar wept and took the boy's hands in his.

"Why didst thou go? and hast thou found the King?" she asked idly, her eyes fixed on the boy's face.

"Yea, we found Him, we adored and at His feet was laid our gifts of gold, frankincense, and myrrh."

"And what gave this new King in return, no amulet whose touch would bring back life."

"He had naught to give, He was divine."

"Divine indeed!" she cried scornfully. "If this be true, then He could cure our child. Hast thou nothing that the King hast touched?"

"Nothing save this," and Caspar reluctantly drew from his bosom a small piece of linen.

She took it and mockingly replied: "It is the linen poor women spin for their children's clothes."

"I begged the linen from His mother, for it had covered the royal head of the Babe and she gave it to me gladly," and Caspar broke in despair.

"They call thee wise," said Ilzaide bitterly, "but I think thou art a fool. Can a piece of linen cure my child? See, I throw thy precious rag away."

In her excitement, the precious cloth fell from her hand on the body of the boy. As the linen touched him, the boy, who had lain motionless for hours, moved, a shudder ran through his body, and he opened his eyes, and smiled—virtue had come from the clothing of the King.

"I was wrong. If thou hast not followed that star our son had died," wept Ilzaide. "Oh, blessed star, whose shining has brought such joy into this house."

"The star," repeated Caspar, and his gaze grew fixed. While for a moment, in place of his son on the couch, he saw the little Babe in far-away Bethlehem wrapped in swaddling clothes and laid in a manger.

O star of wonder, star of night, Star with royal beauty bright, Westward leading, still proceeding, Guide us to thy perfect light.

—John Henry Hopkins Jr.

Opposite: *Angel with Lute*, Rosso Fiorentino, 1495–1540.

We
saw the light
shine out
a-far,
On
Christmas
in the
morning,
And straight
we knew
Christ's
Star
it was,
Bright
beaming in
the morning.

THE BOY WITHOUT A NAME

W. Bardsley Brash
British Weekly January 1, 1931

Long, long ago there was a boy who worked at an inn. We know not his name; but we will tell you a story about him. He was the boy-of-all-work. It was his task to look after the cattle, and to do odd jobs at the inn. There came a time when there was a great stir at this inn, for the little town was full of pilgrims, and the inn was overcrowded. A number of folk wanted lodgings, and they sought for them, and found them not. Amongst these was a tired woman and a man with a troubled look. The stable boy heard them pleading with the landlord. The landlord was kind but firm, and said, "I should like to take you into the inn, but it is quite impossible. I have already turned many away." The man and the woman pleaded, but to no avail. The lad of the inn heard the eager request and the firm refusal, and his heart was strangely stirred. He slipped away from them and said to himself, "They will find their way to the stable. I will make it sweet and clean for them." So he ran speedily and made everything as tidy as possible, and put clean, fresh, sweet-smelling hay in the manger, and then went back to the inn, for there was much work for him to do there.

Some time after he slipped out of the inn and beheld a strange light in the wind-swept shed. There he saw the two tired pilgrims, and, O wonder of wonders, a babe—lying in a manger in the warm, fresh, sweet-smelling hay. All was clean, tidy and homely, and the man and the woman and the child looked so happy. The boy was so merry and said, "I put the hay there on which the baby sleeps. No one knows; it is better when nobody knows." Back again he ran to his work, and whistled for sheer joy as he bustled about, answering the quick calls of the many people at the inn. Night fell—a clear night, full of stars. The boy slipped out of the inn and ran to the stable. He said, "I should just like one more peep before I go to sleep." Amazement fell upon him. There were, O wonder of wonders, shepherds kneeling, and they were all gazing with joyous astonishment at the babe lying in the manger. They spoke of the heavenly light, of the song of angels, of tidings of great joy to all people. No one noticed the boy of the inn, for he hid himself in the darkness. But he saw all, and as he lay down to rest he said, "I placed the hay there for the wonderful child. No one knows; it is better when nobody knows."

The next day the boy of the inn was busy—all the world seemed calling for him, for the inn was crowded, and the pilgrims needed so many things. He had no time during the day to go to the manger, but as he ran to and fro on his errands he saw the vision of a babe, lying on clean, fresh, sweet-smelling hay. He was so glad that he had brought the hay, that he had placed it in the manger, and that the child slept sweetly in this soft bed. He longed to see the babe again, but not until night was he able. Then swiftly he ran, and, O wonder of wonders, he saw kingly pilgrims, swarthy of face, kneeling in lowly adoration before the manger. They talked of a star they had seen in the East, of long journeys over burning sands, and of the wondrous joy which was theirs in worshipping the babe. They brought forth beautiful gifts—gold, frankincense and myrrh—and these, they said, were gifts for the babe. The strange light in the stable made the precious jewels flash with heavenly splendour. The little boy kneeled in the shadows, and worshiped and rejoiced, and said, "What beautiful gifts! . . . but mine was *first,* for I came before the shepherds and the distant travellers, and tidied the stable, and brought the present of clean, fresh, sweet-smelling hay. I am glad that I was the first to bring a gift, and that love led me to make a warm bed for the kingly babe. No one knows; it is better when nobody knows." And no man or woman or child would ever have known had not an angel told me this Christmastide the story; but even he did not mention the name of the dear boy, but always called him "the boy without a name."

Then did we fall on bended knee,
On Christmas in the morning,
And prais'd the Lord, who'd let us see
His glory at its dawning.

—Old English Carol

Le Marchand,
E. Sachsse, 1850.

GIFTS OF CHRISTMAS

Befana is the Italian Christmas gift giver. Her name may derive from the word EPIPHANY, for it is on that day that she has traditionally been active. Befana is an old woman, dressed in black and carrying a broom. Because she missed the chance to travel to Bethlehem with the Magi to worship the newborn Jesus, she is forever wandering in search of the manger, carrying her gifts for the Child. Each January 6, she distributes some of these gifts to the good children of Italy. Those who have not lived up to expectations get only a bag of ashes.

The book COLLECTANEA ET FLORES, which was credited to The Venerable Bede of around A.D. 735, first records a legend of the wise men's names and appearance. In this writing, Bede called the first MELCHIOR, an old man with white hair and a long beard bringing gold. The second was GASPAR, young with a ruddy complexion, who brought incense. The third, of black complexion, was called BALTHAZAR and brought myrrh.

Tradition says there were three Magi because of the three gifts. The Christians in the Orient held a tradition of twelve Magi, and in early paintings and mosaics they were represented as four or even more.

In Russia, BABOUSHKA, or Grandmother, brings children gifts. According to story, she repented of unkindness and has ever since tried to make amends by distributing gifts to children on Christmas Night.

Thomas Nast invented the concept of Santa Claus. Nast, born in Landau, Germany, son of a Bavarian musician, came to New York City in 1846 at the age of six. He was chief illustrator for HARPER'S WEEKLY and in 1864 did a series of Christmas drawings for the newspaper. Santa's year-round activities are described: his work in making toys and filling stockings, his use of a spyglass to check on young behavior, his decoration of Christmas trees, his trips about the sky in the magic sleigh. Nast died in 1902 in Guayaquil, Ecuador, as U.S. consul appointed by President Theodore Roosevelt.

There are about twenty-four references to St. Nicholas in Washington Irving's DIEDRICH KNICKERBOCKER'S A HISTORY OF NEW YORK. One reference describes St. Nicholas as "laying a finger beside his nose," an attitude picked up by Clement Clarke Moore in "The Night Before Christmas."

The bones of the Magi were supposedly brought from Constantinople to Milan in the sixth century. The Emperor Frederick Barbarossa obtained them in 1164 and brought them to Cologne, where they are enshrined in the great Cathedral of Cologne and remain a special shrine.

The Gospel of Matthew does not tell us much about the Magi. Tradition has made them kings, perhaps because they had a personal audience with King Herod, and because of the following prophetic Bible texts: "The kings of Tarsis and the islands shall offer presents: the kings of the Arabians and of Sheba shall bring gifts" Psalm 71:10. And from Isaiah 60:3, 6 "The kings shall walk in the brightness of thy rising. . . . They shall all come from Sheba, bringing gold and frankincense."

The idea of Santa coming down the chimney came from an old English notion which was that sweeping down the chimney at New Year's was necessary so that good luck could enter in.

ENGRAVINGS BY THOMAS NAST, FROM HARPER'S WEEKLY.

Given,

not lent,

But not

withdrawn—

once sent,

This

Infant

of mankind,

this One,

Is still the

little

welcome

Son.

Opposite: *The Sleigh Ride*,
Hans Zatzka, 1859–1949.

CHRISTMAS WITH THE LITTLE WOMEN

Louisa May Alcott

Where is mother?" asked Meg, as she and Jo ran down to thank her for their gifts, half an hour later.

"Goodness only knows. Some poor creeter come a-beggin', and your ma went straight off to see what was needed. There never *was* such a woman for givin' away vittles and drink, clothes and firin'," replied Hannah, who had lived with the family since Meg was born, and was considered by them all more as a friend than a servant.

"She will be back soon, I think; so fry your cakes, and have everything ready," said Meg, looking over the presents which were collected in a basket and kept under the sofa, ready to be produced at the proper time. "Why, where is Amy's bottle of cologne?" she added as the little flask did not appear.

"She took it a minute ago, and went off with it to put a ribbon on it, or some such notion," replied Jo, dancing about the room to take the first stiffness off the new army slippers.

"How nice my handkerchiefs look, don't they? Hannah washed and ironed them for me, and I marked them all myself," said Beth, looking proudly at the somewhat uneven letters which had cost her such labor.

"Bless the child! She's gone and put 'Mother' on them instead of 'M. March.' How funny!" cried Jo, taking up one.

"Isn't it right? I thought it was better to do it so, because Meg's initials are 'M.M.,' and I don't want anyone to use these but Marmee," said Beth, looking troubled.

"It's all right, dear, and a very pretty idea—quite sensible, too, for no one can ever mistake now. It will please her very much, I know," said Meg, with a frown for Jo and smile for Beth.

"There's mother. Hide the basket, quick!" cried Jo, as a door slammed, and steps sounded in the hall.

Amy came in hastily, and looked rather abashed when she saw her sisters all waiting for her.

"Where have you been, and what are you hiding behind you?" asked Meg, surprised to see, by her hood and cloak, that lazy Amy had been out so early.

"Don't laugh at me, Jo! I didn't mean anyone should know till the time came. I only meant to change the little bottle for a big one, and I gave all my money to get it, and I'm truly trying not to be selfish any more."

New
every year,
New-born
and newly
dear,
He comes
with tidings
and a
song,
The ages
long, the
ages
long.

Even
as the cold
Keen winter
grows
not old
As childhood
is so fresh,
foreseen,
And spring in
the familiar
green.

As she spoke, Amy showed the handsome flask which replaced the cheap one; and looked so earnest and humble in her little effort to forget herself that Meg hugged her on the spot, and Jo pronounced her "a trump," while Beth ran to the window, and picked her finest rose to ornament the stately bottle.

"You see I felt ashamed of my present, after reading and talking about being good this morning, so I ran round the corner and changed it the minute I was up; and I'm *so* glad, for mine is the handsomest now."

Another bang of the street door sent the basket under the sofa, and the girls to the table, eager for breakfast.

"Merry Christmas, Marmee! Many of them! Thank you for our books; we read some, and mean to every day," they cried, in chorus.

"Merry Christmas, little daughters! I'm glad you began at once, and hope you will keep on. But I want to say one word before we sit down. Not far away from here lies a poor woman with a little newborn baby. Six children are huddled into one bed to keep from freezing, for they have

La Place De La Republique,
Paris, Eugene Galien-Laloue,
1854–1941.

no fire. There is nothing to eat over there; and the oldest boy came to tell me they were suffering hunger and cold. My girls, will you give them your breakfast as a Christmas present?"

They were all unusually hungry, having waited nearly an hour, and for a minute no one spoke; only a minute, for Jo exclaimed impetuously:

"I'm so glad you came before we began!"

"May I go and help carry the things to the poor little children?" asked Beth eagerly.

"*I* shall take the cream and the muffins," added Amy, heroically giving up the articles she most liked.

Meg was already covering the buckwheats, and piling the bread into one big plate.

"I thought you'd do it," said Mrs. March, smiling as if satisfied. "You shall all go and help me, and when we come back we will have bread and milk for breakfast, and make it up at dinnertime."

They were soon ready, and the procession set out. Fortunately it was early, and they went through back streets, so few people saw them, and no one laughed at the queer party.

A poor, bare, miserable room it was, with broken windows, no fire, ragged bedclothes, a sick mother, wailing baby, and a group of pale, hungry children cuddled under one old quilt, trying to keep warm.

How the big eyes stared and the blue lips smiled as the girls went in!

"*Ach, mein Gott!* It is good angels come to us!" said the poor woman, crying for joy.

"Funny angels in hoods and mittens," said Jo, and set them laughing.

In a few minutes it really did seem as if kind spirits had been at work there. Hannah, who had carried wood, made a fire, and stopped up the broken panes with old hats and her own cloak. Mrs. March gave the mother tea and gruel, and comforted her with promises of help, while she dressed the little baby as tenderly as if it had been her own. The girls, meantime, spread the table, set the children round the fire, and fed them like so many hungry birds—laughing, talking, and trying to understand the funny broken English.

"*Das ist gut!*" "*Die Engel-kinder!*" cried the poor things, as they ate, and warmed their purple hands at the comfortable blaze.

The girls had never been called angel children before, and thought it very agreeable. . . . That was a very happy breakfast, though they didn't get any of it; and when they went away, leaving comfort behind, I think there were not in all the city four merrier people than the hungry little girls who gave away their breakfasts and contented themselves with bread and milk on Christmas morning.

Sudden
as sweet
Come the
expected
feet,
All
joy
is young,
and new
all
art,
And He, too,
whom we
have by
heart.

—Alice Meynell

The children
dreamed
the whole
night through
Of stockings
hung the
hearth
beside;
And bound
to make
each
dream
come true
Went Santa
Claus at
Christmas-tide.

FROM DIEDRICH KNICKERBOCKER'S A HISTORY OF NEW YORK

Washington Irving

Nor must I omit to record one of the earliest measures of this infant settlement, inasmuch as it shows the piety of our forefathers, and that, like good Christians, they were always ready to serve God after they had first served themselves. Thus, having quietly settled themselves down and provided for their own comfort, they bethought themselves of testifying their gratitude to the great and good St. Nicholas for his protecting care in guiding them to this delectable abode. To this end, they built a fair and goodly chapel within the fort, which they consecrated to his name; whereupon he immediately took the town of New Amsterdam under his peculiar patronage, and he has ever since been and I devoutly hope will ever be, the titular saint of this excellent city. . . .

At this early period was instituted that pious ceremony, still religiously observed in all our ancient families of the right breed, of hanging up a stocking in the chimney on St. Nicholas eve; which stocking is always found in the morning miraculously filled—for the good St. Nicholas has ever been a great giver of gifts, particularly to children. . . .

And as of yore, in the better days of man, the dieties were wont to visit him on earth and bless his rural habitations, so, we are told, in the sylvan days of New Amsterdam, the good St. Nicholas would often make his appearance in his beloved city, of a holiday afternoon, riding jollily among the treetops, or over the roofs of the houses, now and then drawing forth magnificent presents from his breeches pockets, and dripping them down the chimneys of his favorites. Whereas, in these days of iron and brass, he never shows us the light of his countenance, nor ever visits us, save one night in the year, when he rattles down the chimneys of the descendants of patriarchs, confining his presents merely to the children.

Opposite: *Father Christmas*,
Karl Roger.

Black
stockings,
red, brown,
white and
gray—
Long, little,
warm,
or patched and
thin—
The kindly
saint
found on his
way,
And, smiling,
popped his
presents in.

—Marguerite
Merington

GOOD SAINT NICK

Maymie Richardson Krythe

There's a
jolly little
fellow
Who come
riding into
town.
When the
north wind
blows his
trumpet,
And the
snow comes
dancing
down;

For many centuries, "Good Saint Nick"—Saint Nicholas or Santa Claus to American children—the patron saint of young people, has been associated with Christmas and gifts. His name, originally from the Latin, *Sanctus Nicolaus,* has had various forms, including the German, *Sankt Nikolaus,* Dutch *Sinter Klaas,* finally becoming our modern "Santa Claus." Although it is customary to regard him as a myth, there actually was a real St. Nicholas, an early Christian bishop, who lived during the fourth century. It was because of his unusual generosity that our ideas of the modern saint have developed.

Nicholas, the only child of wealthy Christian parents, was born at the close of the third century, perhaps about 280, at Patara, a port in the province of Lycia in Asia Minor. Early in his childhood, his devout mother taught him the Scriptures. When both parents died during an epidemic, they left the young boy in possession of all their wealth.

Young Nicholas dedicated his life to God's service and moved to Myra, chief city of his province. There, after the death of their bishop, members of the Council balloted unsuccessfully, for some time, trying to choose a successor. Finally, in a dream, the oldest official was told to stand next day at the cathedral door and select as the new bishop the first man named Nicholas who entered.

When the young Christian went to church as usual for morning prayers, he was asked his name; and soon afterward he was selected by the Council and consecrated to the high office. Nicholas, because of his youth, tried to refuse the position, but he was overruled.

Early in his new career, during a visit to the Holy Land, he was so impressed by the places connected with Christ's life that he decided to resign from his bishopric at Myra and remain in Palestine. But God commanded him to return to Asia Minor. During the reign of Emperor Diocletian, when many Christians were persecuted, the young bishop was imprisoned, in the year 303. Later he was freed, when Constantine the Great "proclaimed an imperial toleration of all religions."

Nicholas was very popular as bishop, and several stories of his ability to perform miracles have come down to us. On his return from the Holy

Land, it is said that a mighty storm arose, and the ship was almost wrecked. Nicholas calmly prayed to God; and the sailors were astonished when the wind suddenly abated, and their lives and ship were saved. . . .

One of Nicholas's chief characteristics was his unsurpassed generosity. In his youth he had learned, by going around among the people, how many were oppressed by poverty. As a result, he often went out in disguise and distributed presents, especially to children.

The most popular story of the saint's good deeds concerned the three daughters of a nobleman who had lost his fortune in unsuccessful business ventures. As a result, there was no money for dowries; and in those days, a daughter without a dowry had little chance for marriage.

The bishop decided to remedy this; and when the oldest girl was of marriageable age, he went to their home one night and secretly threw a bag of gold through the window. Not long afterward, the girl married well; and at the proper time for the second, Nicholas repeated his kind deed.

But when the third was grown, her father decided to keep a close watch to find out who their benefactor was. When he caught the bishop in the very act of throwing in the bag of money, the grateful father could not keep the secret, even though the donor begged him not to reveal his name. So the three daughters were happily married, all through the kindness and generosity of St. Nicholas, who is consequently regarded as the patron of marriageable girls.

One version of this story is that one of the purses or bags fell into a stocking hung near the chimney to dry and that, from this incident, the Christmas custom of hanging stockings in anticipation of receiving presents originated. Stories of the bishop's liberality soon spread; and, thereafter, when unexpected gifts were received, he was given credit as the donor.

After the bishop's death in 341 (or near that date) there was sincere mourning for him. Stories of his generosity and miracles were told far and wide; and pilgrims came from long distances to visit his burial place.

In a coat of
fur
and ermine,
He is muffled
to his
chin,
And his face,
whate'er the
weather,
Always wears
a pleasant
grin.

CHRISTMAS LONG AGO

Theodore Ledyard Cuyler

He's a friend
of all the
children
For he carries
on his back
Gifts to make
the bright eyes
sparkle
Safely stowed
within his
pack;

As the visits of Santa Claus in the night could only be through the chimney, we hung our stockings where they would be in full sight. Three score and ten years ago such modern contrivances as steam pipes, and those unpoetical holes in the floor called "hot-air registers," were as entirely unknown in our rural regions as gas-burners or telephones. We had a genuine fire-place in our kitchen, big enough to contain an enormous back-log, and broad enough for eight or ten people to form "a circle wide" before it and enjoy the genial warmth.

The last process before going to bed was to suspend our stockings in the chimney jambs; and then we dreamed of Santa Claus, or if we awoke in the night, we listened for the jingling of his sleighbells. At the peep of day we were aroused by the voice of my good grandfather, who planted himself in the stairway and shouted in a stentorian tone, "I wish you all a Merry Christmas!" The contest was as to who should give the salutation first, and the old gentleman determined to get the start of us by sounding his greeting to the family before we were out of our rooms. Then came a race for the chimney corner; all the stockings came down quicker than they had gone up. What could not be contained in them was disposed upon the mantelpiece, or elsewhere. I remember that I once received an autograph letter from Santa Claus, full of good counsels; and our . . . cook told me that she awoke in the night and, peeping into the kitchen, actually saw the veritable old visitor light a candle and sit down at the table and write it! I believed it all as implicitly as I believed the Ten Commandments, or the story of David and Goliath.

Opposite: *Three Children by Fireplace*,
Artist Unknown.

And they
always hang
their
stockings
By the fireplace
because
Christmas Eve
is sure to bring
them
Presents
from old
Santa Claus.

—Author Unknown

He comes
in the
night!
He comes in
the night!
He softly,
silently
comes;
While the
little brown
heads
on the pillows
so white
Are dreaming
of bugles and
drums.

A Visit from St. Nicholas

Clement Clarke Moore inadvertently defined an American image of Santa Claus when he wrote a short poem entitled "A Visit from St. Nicholas." Moore wrote the poem as a holiday gift to his children while riding in his sleigh to his estate outside of New York City. Moore was a professor of Oriental and Greek literature at Columbia University where he was known for his serious writings on religion, literature, and education. He was, however, also the father of nine children; and on that snowy evening in late December of 1822, he was thinking of a way to delight his children as they gathered around him on Christmas Eve.

The legend of St. Nicholas had been part of Christmas lore throughout the world for centuries. The Dutch who settled in New York brought St. Nicholas to America, but he did not become truly American until Moore fashioned for him a new identity. The physical traits Moore attributed to St. Nicholas were, ironically, modeled after an old Dutch handyman who worked on the family estate.

Moore never sought publication for his poem, never wished to have it read outside his home, and, for almost a quarter of a century, refused to publicly acknowledge authorship. A meddling friend ignored Moore's wishes to keep his poem in the family and sent it to a newspaper where it was anonymously published just before Christmas 1823. Within a few years, the poem became well known in almost every American home. From that time on, "The Night Before Christmas" found a place in the heart of every American child who cherished the hopes and dreams of Christmas.

'Twas the night before Christmas, when all through the house
Not a creature was stirring, not even a mouse;
The stockings were hung by the chimney with care,
In hopes that St. Nicholas soon would be there;
The children were nestled all snug in their beds,
While visions of sugar-plums danced through their heads;
And mamma in her kerchief, and I in my cap,
Had just settled our brains for a long winter's nap,—
When out on the lawn there arose such a clatter,
I sprang from my bed to see what was the matter.
Away to the window I flew like a flash,
Tore open the shutters and threw up the sash.
The moon, on the breast of the new-fallen snow,
Gave a lustre of midday to objects below;
When what to my wondering eyes should appear,

But a miniature sleigh and eight tiny reindeer,
With a little old driver so lively and quick
I knew in a moment it must be St. Nick.
More rapid than eagles his coursers they came,
And he whistled and shouted and called them by name:
"Now, Dasher! now, Dancer! now, Prancer and Vixen!
On, Comet! on, Cupid! on, Donder and Blitzen!
To the top of the porch, to the top of the wall!
Now, dash away, dash away, dash away all!"
As dry leaves that before the wild hurricane fly,
When they meet with an obstacle, mount to the sky,
So, up to the house-top the coursers they flew,
With a sleigh full of toys,—and St. Nicholas too.
And then in a twinkling I heard on the roof
The prancing and pawing of each little hoof.
As I drew in my head and was turning around,
Down the chimney St. Nicholas came with a bound.
He was dressed all in fur from his head to his foot,
And his clothes were all tarnished with ashes and soot;
A bundle of toys he had flung on his back,
And he looked like a peddler just opening his pack.
His eyes how they twinkled! his dimples how merry!
His cheeks were like roses, his nose like a cherry;
His droll little mouth was drawn up like a bow,
And the beard on his chin was as white as the snow.
The stump of a pipe he held tight in his teeth,
And the smoke it encircled his head like a wreath.
He had a broad face, and a little round belly
That shook, when he laughed, like a bowl full of jelly.
He was chubby and plump,—a right jolly old elf—
And I laughed when I saw him, in spite of myself.
A wink of his eye and a twist of his head
Soon gave me to know I had nothing to dread.
He spoke not a word, but went straight to his work,
And filled all the stockings; then turned with a jerk,
And laying his finger aside of his nose,
And giving a nod, up the chimney he rose.
He sprang to his sleigh, to his team gave a whistle,
And away they all flew like the down of a thistle;
But I heard him exclaim, ere he drove out of sight:
"Happy Christmas to all, and to all a good-night!"

He cuts through the snow like a ship through the foam, While the white flakes around him whirl; Who tells him I know not, but he findeth the home Of each good little boy and girl.

—Author Unknown

Bid them
come, not, as
of old, With
frankincense,
myrrh,
gems and
gold, But
with the
nobler—
love's own
proffer—
Unto their
God their
hearts to offer.

—Kathleen
Kavanagh

Opposite: *Music of a Bygone Age,*
John Melhuish Strudwick, 1849–1937.

THE BALLAD OF BEFANA

Phyllis McGinley

Befana the Housewife, scrubbing her pane,
Saw three old sages ride down the lane,
Saw three gray travelers pass her door—
Gaspar, Balthazar, Melchior.

"Where journey you, sirs?" she asked of them.
Balthazar answered, "To Bethlehem,

For we have news of a marvelous thing.
Born in a stable is Christ the King."

"Give Him my welcome!" Then Gaspar smiled,
"Come with us, mistress, to greet the Child."

"Oh, happily, happily would I fare,
Were my dusting through and I'd polished the stair."

Old Melchior leaned on his saddle horn.
"Then send but a gift to the small Newborn."

"Oh, gladly, gladly I'd send Him one,
Were the hearthstone swept and my weaving done.

"As soon as ever I've baked my bread,
I'll fetch Him a pillow for His head,
And a coverlet too," Befana said.

"When the rooms are aired and the linen dry,
I'll look at the Babe."
But the Three rode by.

She worked for a day and a night and a day,
Then, gifts in her hands, took up her way.
But she never could find where the Christ Child lay.

And still she wanders at Christmastide,
Houseless, whose house was all her pride,

Whose heart was tardy, whose gifts were late;
Wanders, and knocks at every gate,
Crying, "Good people, the bells begin!
Put off your toiling and let love in."

A Christmas
gift
love
sends to thee,
'Tis not a
gift
that you
may see,
Like
frankincense
or shining
gold,
Yet 'tis a gift
that you
may hold.

THE GIFT OF THE MAGI

O. Henry

William Sydney Porter, the author of the Christmas story "The Gift of the Magi," began his writing career in prison. Incarcerated for three years on charges of embezzlement, charges which he always denied, Porter began writing to fill the empty hours. In 1904, he published his first collection of stories, under the name O. Henry. Critics were hesitant to take him seriously and called his work unsophisticated and predictable; but the public held no such reservations, and many of O. Henry's stories became widely popular, especially "The Gift of the Magi." The story describes a Christmastime in the lives of a young couple named Jim and Della, who are nearly destitute, but profoundly in love and caught up in the spirit of Christmas. Both worry about how to afford a proper present for the other, and each sacrifices that which is closest to his or her heart to please the other. A simple tale with a compelling message, O. Henry's "The Gift of the Magi" has proven to be truly timeless.

Now, there were two possessions of the James Dillingham Youngs in which they both took a mighty pride. One was Jim's gold watch that had been his father's and his grandfather's. The other was Della's hair. Had the Queen of Sheba lived in the flat across the air shaft, Della would have let her hair hang out the window someday to dry just to depreciate her Majesty's jewels and gifts. Had King Solomon been the janitor, with all his treasures piled up in the basement, Jim would have pulled out his watch every time he passed, just to see him pluck at his beard from envy.

So now Della's beautiful hair fell about her, rippling and shining like a cascade of brown waters. It reached below her knee and made itself almost a garment for her. And then she did it up again nervously and quickly. Once she faltered for a minute and stood still while a tear or two splashed on the worn red carpet.

On went her old brown jacket; on went her old brown hat. With a whirl of skirts and with the brilliant sparkle still in her eyes, she fluttered out the door and down the stairs to the street.

Where she stopped and read the sign: "Mme. Sofronie. Hair Goods of All Kinds." One flight up Della ran, and collected herself, panting. Madame, large, too white, chilly, hardly looked the "Sofronie."

"Will you buy my hair?" asked Della.

"I buy hair," said Madame. "Take yer hat off and let's have a sight at the looks of it."

Down rippled the brown cascade.

"Twenty dollars," said Madame, lifting the mass with a practiced hand.

"Give it to me quick," said Della.

Oh, and the next two hours tripped by on rosy wings. Forget the hashed metaphor. She was ransacking the stores for Jim's present.

She found it at last. It surely had been made for Jim and no one else. There was no other like it in any of the stores, and she had turned all of them inside out. It was a platinum fob chain, simple and chaste in design, properly proclaiming its value by substance alone and not by meretricious ornamentation—as all good things should do. It was even worthy of The Watch. As soon as she saw it she knew that it must be Jim's. It was like him. Quietness and value—the description applied to both. Twenty-one dollars they took from her for it, and she hurried home with the eighty-seven cents. With that chain on his watch Jim might be properly anxious about the time in any company. Grand as the watch was, he sometimes looked at it on the sly on account of the old leather strap that he used in place of a chain.

When Della reached home her intoxication gave way a little to prudence and reason. She got out her curling irons and lighted the gas and went to work repairing the ravages made by generosity added to love. Which is always a tremendous task, dear friends—a mammoth task.

Within forty minutes her head was covered with tiny close-lying curls that made her look wonderfully like a truant schoolboy. She looked at her reflection in the mirror long, carefully, and critically.

"If Jim doesn't kill me," she said to herself, "before he takes a second look at me, he'll say I look like a Coney Island chorus girl. But what could I do—oh! what could I do with a dollar and eighty-seven cents?"

At seven o'clock the coffee was made and the frying pan was on the back of the stove, hot and ready to cook the chops.

Jim was never late. Della doubled the fob chain in her hand and sat on the corner of the table near the door that he always entered. Then she heard his step on the stair away down on the first flight, and she turned white for just a moment. She had a habit of saying little silent prayers about the simplest everyday things, and now she whispered: "Please, God, make him think I am still pretty."

The door opened and Jim stepped in and closed it. He looked thin and very serious. Poor fellow, he was only twenty-two—and to be burdened with a family! He needed a new overcoat and he was without gloves.

If you are
lacking
bread
and meat,
'Twill
give you
Heavenly
bread to eat,
If you are
down-trod,
e'en as Job,
'Twill
dress
you in a
seamless robe.

The gift
of Love in
Mary's eyes,
Looked down
on Jesus with
surprise,
That one so
great,
should be so
small,
To point the
way for
kings,
and all.

Jim stopped inside the door, as immovable as a setter at the scent of quail. His eyes were fixed upon Della, and there was an expression in them that she could not read, and it terrified her. It was not anger, nor surprise, nor disapproval, nor horror, nor any of the sentiments that she had been prepared for. He simply stared at her fixedly with that peculiar expression on his face.

Della wriggled off the table and went for him.

"Jim, darling," she cried, "don't look at me that way. I had my hair cut off and sold it because I couldn't have lived through Christmas without giving you a present. It'll grow out again—you won't mind, will you? I just had to do it. My hair grows awfully fast. Say 'Merry Christmas!' Jim, and let's be happy. You don't know what a nice—what a beautiful, nice gift I've got for you."

"You've cut off your hair?" asked Jim laboriously, as if he had not arrived at that patent fact yet even after the hardest mental labor.

"Cut it off and sold it," said Della. "Don't you like me just as well anyhow? I'm me without my hair, ain't I?"

Jim looked about the room curiously.

"You say your hair is gone?" he said, with an air almost of idiocy.

"You needn't look for it," said Della. "It is sold. I tell you—sold and gone, too. It's Christmas Eve, boy. Be good to me, for it went for you. Maybe the hairs of my head were numbered," she went on with a sudden serious sweetness, "but nobody could ever count my love for you. Shall I put the chops on, Jim?"

Out of his trance Jim seemed quickly to wake. He enfolded his Della. For ten seconds let us regard with discreet scrutiny some inconsequential object in the other direction. Eight dollars a week or a million a year—what is the difference? A mathematician or a wit would give you the wrong answer. The magi brought valuable gifts, but that was not among them. This dark assertion will be illuminated later on.

Jim drew a package from his overcoat pocket and threw it upon the table.

"Don't make any mistake, Dell," he said, "about me. I don't think there's anything in the way of a haircut or a shave or a shampoo that could make me like my girl any less. But if you'll unwrap that package you may see why you had me going awhile at first."

White fingers and nimble tore at the string and paper. And then an ecstatic scream of joy; and then alas! a quick feminine change to hysterical tears and wails, necessitating the immediate employment of all the comforting powers of the lord of the flat.

For there lay The Combs—the set of combs, side and back, that Della had worshiped for long in a Broadway window. Beautiful combs, pure tortoiseshell, with jeweled rims—just the shade to wear in the beautiful vanished hair. They were expensive combs, she knew, and her heart had simply craved and yearned over them without the least hope of possession. And now they were hers, but the tresses that should have adorned the coveted adornments were gone.

But she hugged them to her bosom, and at length she was able to look up with dim eyes and a smile and say, "My hair grows so fast, Jim!"

And then Della leaped up like a little singed cat and cried, "Oh, oh!"

Jim had not yet seen his beautiful present. She held it out to him eagerly upon her open palm. The dull precious metal seemed to flash with a reflection of her bright and ardent spirit.

"Isn't it a dandy, Jim? I hunted all over town to find it. You'll have to look at the time a hundred times a day now. Give me your watch. I want to see how it looks on it."

Instead of obeying, Jim tumbled down on the couch and put his hands under the back of his head and smiled.

"Dell," said he, "let's put our Christmas presents away and keep 'em awhile. They're too nice to use just at present. I sold the watch to get the money to buy your combs. And now suppose you put the chops on."

The magi, as you know, were wise men—wonderfully wise men—who brought gifts to the Babe in the manger. They invented the art of giving Christmas presents. Being wise, their gifts were no doubt wise ones, possibly bearing the privilege of exchange in case of duplication. And here I have lamely related to you the uneventful chronicle of two foolish children in a flat who most unwisely sacrificed for each other the greatest treasures of their house. But in a last word to the wise of these days let it be said that of all who give gifts these two were the wisest. Of all who give and receive gifts, such as they are wisest. Everywhere they are wisest. They are the magi.

One heart of Love can move the race, One grain of truth can change earth's face, A Bethlehem babe, a shepherd's rod, Have lifted mankind up to God.

—Clarence Hawkes

Come, we shepherds,
whose blest sight Hath
met Love's moon in
nature's night;
Come, lift we up our
loftier song,
And wake the sun that
lies too long!
Gloomy night embrace
the place Where the
noble Infant lay
The Babe looked up and
showed His face;
In spite of darkness,
it was day.

—Richard Crashaw

*The Nativity with Angels Adoring
the Christ Child*, Charles Poerson,
1609–1667.

INDEX

PHOTOGRAPHY CREDITS